How
to
Listen

An Hachette UK Company
www.hachette.co.uk

First published in Great Britain in 2021 by Kyle Books,
an imprint of Octopus Publishing Group Limited
Carmelite House
50 Victoria Embankment
London EC4Y 0DZ

ISBN: 978 0 85783 940 4

Distributed in the US by Hachette Book Group, 1290 Avenue of the Americas,
4th and 5th Floors, New York, NY 10104

Distributed in Canada by Canadian Manda Group, 664 Annette St., Toronto,
Ontario, Canada M6S 2C8

Editorial Director: Judith Hannam
Publisher: Joanna Copestick
Assistant Editor: Florence Filose
Copy Editor: Tara O'Sullivan
Design: Steve Leard
Watercolour: Shutterstock
Production: Katherine Hockley

A Cataloguing in Publication record for this title is available
from the British Library.

Printed and bound in the Czech Republic

10 9 8 7 6 5 4 3 2 1

Katie Colombus

How
to
Listen

Tools for opening up
conversations when
it matters most

Contents

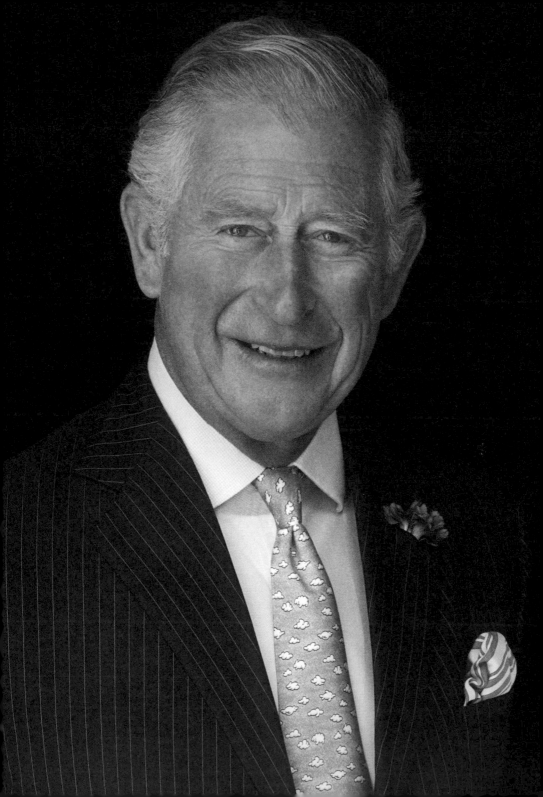

For over twenty years I have been proud to be the Patron of Samaritans, supporting the charity's aim of assisting those in emotional crisis.

On 2nd November 1953, Chad Varah, a vicar and writer-cartoonist, answered the first ever call to a new helpline for people troubled with thoughts of taking their own life. He and his wife had been offering counselling to parishioners, but they wanted to do something more to help people in intense emotional distress. And so, from the parish of St Stephen Walbrook in the City of London, they started taking anonymous calls with the intention of listening with empathy and without judgement.

Chad Varah took out a newspaper advertisement asking for volunteers who would use "active listening therapy". The idea was considered quite radical – because of course at this time the act of suicide was a criminal offence. He let the volunteers sit with clients waiting for a counselling appointment, and often found that the clients would pour out their problems to the volunteers themselves and so felt no need to speak to him afterwards. The power of those listening volunteers turned out to be the real strength of the service.

Today, Samaritans has over 20,000 volunteers and 201 branches across the United Kingdom and Ireland. And every six seconds, a Samaritan responds to a call for help. The 24-hour listening service has come to be all that Chad Varah envisioned – and far more. Each year Samaritans reach over half a million people via a 24-hour service, delivered by phone, email, letter, face to face and through a Welsh language service, as well as through work in schools, prisons, hospitals and local communities.

I am immensely proud of the volunteers and staff who work so tirelessly, day and night to provide this essential care to so many vulnerable people who often feel they have nowhere else to turn.

By using the Samaritans' compassionate model of active listening, it is my sincere hope that we can all become better listeners. We all have it within us to be present for our loved ones, friends, family and colleagues, in times of darkness and despair, and to use our natural skills of listening with compassion to help others when they need it most.

Preface:
Listen and learn

I've travelled all over the world and listening has been, for me, the most important learning tool of all. Listening doesn't just mean a few moments of polite attention before you get on to what you want to say; listening means being prepared to take the time to tune in to another life. It isn't always easy.

Listening well requires the patience to stay with someone who may not be able to articulate exactly what they are feeling, and to be able to assure whoever you're listening to that they are the most important person in your life at that moment.

A good listener knows that silence can sometimes say far more than words. A good listener is never judgemental. Be prepared for difficult, sometimes angry and ungrateful responses, but try to understand the context from which they come.

Most of all, listening requires you to forget your own ego, to set aside your own preoccupations and anxieties, and to give your full concentration to whoever's speaking to you. The rewards are that a good listener can change someone's life – even save someone's life. And who knows? That life could be your own.

Michael Palin, Samaritans supporter

This book

By incorporating Samaritans' listening principles into your everyday life, you will be able to better recognise when those close to you need to talk, and you'll have enough confidence to approach a difficult conversation. This book is a collection of stories, tips, practical exercises and guidance from listening volunteers and experts, as well as people whose lives have been changed by the power of listening, many of whom now use their experiences to help others as Samaritans volunteers, or work as clinical psychologists or in other professions where they can provide care and support. We will explore their ideas and advice, from learning about how feeling heard can provide relief, reassurance and validation, to discovering fascinating facts about brain chemistry.

We want you to listen to one another – to friends, family, colleagues, partners, neighbours, whoever you like – in the hope that not so many people end up feeling they have nowhere else to turn. By becoming a nation of listeners, we can work towards supporting and enhancing each other's emotional wellbeing and reducing the stigma around mental health. We all have it within ourselves to listen better to those we care about. Sometimes all we need is a little confidence and reassurance in order to feel able to reach out and start a conversation about how someone might be feeling.

PART ONE

Why Listening Matters

'There are, in this world, people who seem to be "ordinary", but who turn out to be extraordinary. They give their total attention. They listen and listen and listen, without interrupting. They do not preach. They have nothing to sell. We call them Samaritans.'

Chad Varah,
founder of Samaritans

Chapter 1:
Why listening is important

Pause for a moment and try to remember the last time you had a really good conversation with someone. It might have been at work, at home or in the pub. It could have been with a friend, colleague or family member. It might even have been with your local coffee barista or delivery driver. But what was it that made that conversation so memorable?

Did the person give you their undivided attention? Did they look directly at you, make eye contact and make you feel seen? Did they let you speak, without interruption, not cutting in to offer advice, but rather allowing you the freedom to express whatever it was you wanted to say – really making you feel heard?

Now think about another conversation you've had recently where you didn't feel so listened to. Perhaps you got the feeling that the person you were talking to was just waiting for you to finish speaking so that they could give you an opinion on what you'd just said, offer some advice or tell you about a time when something like that had happened to them. Conversations like this can feel as though they are made up of two people jostling for air space – each person listening for just long enough until it's their turn to speak.

Most of the time, conversing is a two-way street, with a lot of give and take, so it doesn't always come naturally to us to enter a conversation with the intention of listening rather than replying. On top of this, life is full of busy distractions. It can often be difficult to feel heard. But this is why it's so important to find the right time and place for listening and having a good, meaningful conversation.

At times, we all need to get something off our chests and have those long, winding conversations that end up somewhere unexpected. It might be that we need a good vent, or simply a chat to relieve boredom, lift the spirits and take our minds off the day we've had. But sometimes there could be more going on with someone, and you might feel like it's time to have a deeper and more meaningful conversation, perhaps about a potentially sensitive or challenging topic. And you might worry that it won't be easy – either for you, or for them.

Listening can remind someone you care

Often, when talking to someone about their day-to-day stresses and strains, just saying 'Are you OK?' can be enough to remind someone that you care – those three little words can make a really big difference. But if someone you know well is feeling low, suffering emotional pain, going through something that feels overwhelming, complicated and distressing, or has an ongoing mental health issue, then active listening can really help. Active listening is more than just hearing somebody: it involves really concentrating on what the other person is saying and carefully considering the points they are making, without interrupting or offering your own opinion. Lending an ear with empathy, and without judgement or advice, can be the most effective means of really helping the person you are talking to. Listening to others has an extraordinary ability to make them feel validated, give them back their self-belief and empower them to change the end of their story.

It sounds so simple, doesn't it? And yet this simple act – one that we are all capable of – can make a huge difference to someone's life. For over 65 years now, active listening is a model that has not only worked for Samaritans, but has been described by many as life-saving. We know that helping someone open up and explore their thoughts and feelings can be invaluable. Sometimes it's enough in that moment to simply get everything off their chest; at other times, the conversation can be a catalyst for them to realise they need further help.

Communication is necessary for human survival

Talking – and being heard – is as necessary to humans as breathing, food and water. Speech is one of our first learned skills and it's a key part of our interaction with others. Listening as you learn to communicate is a basic necessity. As we grow, we communicate with our parents, then friends and teachers, then colleagues and family members. The primary function of our speech is a need to be heard, to get our point across, to get the thing that we want – whether we're asking for an ice cream or requesting that a deadline be moved. Because of the practical nature of this primary function, it can dominate over the secondary function of speech – actually being *listened* to.

Listening to someone helps them explore their feelings

Often, when we witness someone we care about going through something difficult, we don't know what to do, or what to say. We want to find a way to help them as soon as we can, and make them feel better. But it can be difficult to know how.

You might try to help them fix the issue by offering advice about their problem, telling them what you once did in a similar situation, giving them tips on what works well for you, or trying to think of a solution. You might judge the situation first, to decide whether or not you agree with them. You might try to use your own experience, seeing the problem from your own point of view and projecting that back on to the person you're speaking with.

A lot of the time, there's absolutely nothing wrong with that – particularly if that person is asking for advice. In normal day-to-day conversations, just airing our concerns can be enough, and sometimes it is useful to be offered a fresh interpretation or an idea that we might not have thought of. Those who know us well are often best placed to reflect on what's worked for us before.

But if the person you're talking to is experiencing anxiety or depression, or dealing with another mental health condition or illness, it can be frustrating for them to hear your viewpoint when, actually, you don't know exactly how they feel, or exactly what they're going through. How can you? We are all different, and so we all react differently. While our collective response to events may be similar, our personal reactions will always be specific to our own experiences. Even if we've been affected by the same kind of things – such as loss or hardship – we will all always behave and respond to them in our own individual ways.

Listening and hearing are two different things

Truly listening to someone in a way that allows them to feel heard is an entirely different experience to simply paying attention while someone talks. It's about taking the time to understand what is really being said, and giving weight and meaning to what you hear. When you listen well, you are reading between the lines, paying full attention and trying to grasp what the other person is really trying to say.

As philosopher Roland Barthes puts it: 'Hearing is a physiological phenomenon; listening is a psychological act.'[1] We are always hearing, most of the time subconsciously – things like the radio, busy streets, background chatter. But listening is a choice. It takes will, concentration and empathy to pay attention to the meaning behind someone's words as opposed to just hearing what is being said. If you really listen with the intent of understanding, rather than that of forming an opinion, or lining up a question in your head while the other person is still talking,

[1] Barthes, Roland. *The Responsibility of Forms*. 1985. Hill and Wang, New York

you will generate a sense of trust that will allow the other person to really feel able to open up to you.

We can all be better listeners

But there are things that stop us from listening well. If we really want to help other people, there are certain challenges which need to be overcome: for example, the overwhelming urge to try and make everything better. When we face a situation where someone we care about is having a hard time, it is natural to feel a strong desire to help. This comes from a good place of love and support, but swooping in to try and fix the situation implies a level of control and dominance that might inadvertently do more harm than good. Most often, the thing that people really want is not for you to try and fix them. They just need you to be there for them.

Casting aside your own beliefs and ingrained knowledge in order to be open enough to listen and accept another's perspective – especially when it conflicts with your own – takes grace, awareness and acceptance.

Samaritans is known for helping people experiencing times of intense emotional crisis and extreme distress. But that's not all we do. A lot of the time, we find that the people who call us are just everyday human beings who are going through something that's really difficult, and so they've ended up in a place where it's hard for them to cope. Our trained volunteers are there to help people in their darkest moments, but they are not therapists who give advice. They are just ordinary people doing something extraordinary.

We know that exploring feelings alleviates distress and helps people reach a better understanding of their situation and the options open to them. We know and accept that we can't fix someone. We can't save them from what they're feeling or going through. Our role is to simply be there alongside them until they are ready to save themselves. It is always our aim that, through listening to someone and giving them the time and space they need to talk things through, that person will make the right choice for themselves. People know their own thoughts better than anyone else, so it makes sense that they are best placed to find their own solutions. Often, they just need help in remembering that.

'When you talk, you are only repeating what you already know. But if you listen, you may learn something new.'

Dalai Lama

Create a safe space

What we do at Samaritans is really simple. It is a natural conversation between two people. The incredible thing is that you can really connect with someone through nothing more than warmth and empathy – it is so powerful. And it has been really valuable for me to get to know and understand people in a different way. Eventually, it becomes part of your day to day, and part of who you are.

That connection between two people is one of the key things you can carry over into more everyday situations. The most important thing we do at Samaritans is create a safe space for people to talk about anything they want, without any fear of judgement. That allows them to really, truly be themselves in a way that they might feel they can't be anywhere else.

Showing empathy is an incredibly important part of reassuring people and creating an environment where people are able to talk openly – and I've learned that this is also true in a more normal, day-to-day context. Just checking in and saying, 'You alright? You don't seem like yourself at the moment,' is a simple, but effective thing to do. It all has to start with paying attention to what your friends and family are going through. At Samaritans, the listening we do is so active that you pick up on every nuance and every pause. You become kind of hypersensitive to what people are saying. I suspect that a lot of things in everyday life go unnoticed because we're not really paying attention to each other. It's not that we don't care, but often we just don't notice the signs or signals that indicate to us that something has been left unsaid or that something's not right.

Being solutions-orientated can often be the biggest barrier for friends and family when it comes to listening to one another, because you've come to a conclusion about what they should do before the person has even finished speaking. But if you try and move away from the idea of finding a solution, then what you're doing is exploring. You're not worrying about what's happening; instead, you are reflecting on what you're hearing and playing it back through a different lens. That's way more helpful to the other person's thought process.

Samaritans training really forces you to rethink how you relate to people, how you think about emotional and mental health and what your role really is. One of the things that stood out for me in my training was being told to imagine someone who's having a hard time, who is feeling depressed or anxious, as if they're sitting in a pit. What friends and family will do, with the best of intentions, is try and help them out of the pit. But as Samaritans, what we do instead is get down into the pit and sit alongside them to explore with them what that feels like. If someone is depressed, they may actually experience the kind of care and help that friends and family try to give them as a form of judgement, because their friends and family want them to be a particular way – to be happy, and feel better, and function normally. Just bringing those ideas into a conversation, consciously or otherwise, is always going to feel like a form of judgement, as if they're being told: 'How you are now isn't quite OK, we need to change it.'

It can help to research and read up on mental health and mental illness – to learn the difference between depression and low mood, or stress and anxiety, or how you would know if someone was bipolar or showing signs of psychosis. It's not about diagnosing: it's about familiarising yourself and trying to accept it for what it is. It will help you with the way you react. It's about taking a deep breath and behaving in a way that will encourage people to talk.

We all play various roles in our lives – friend, colleague, parent, child – and these roles can get in the way of our ability to listen. They often stop us from being on a level playing field, and this can limit our ability to have truly non-judgemental, completely open conversations. One of the fundamental principles for Samaritans is the belief that everyone knows what's best for them. You have to believe that a person will find their own answers when they're ready to, in their own time. You don't know what's right for them. You never really know what people are truly thinking and what they're really worried about. Therefore, the best way to listen and offer support to someone is to show that you care, to show warmth, and to be there. You can provide the safe space that they need and help them to rationalise what's going on for them by talking through their feelings. I think anyone can do it.

If you start with a completely open mind, without any preconceptions or assumptions, other people will see that. If you don't stigmatise mental health in everyday conversations, or casually refer to someone being 'a bit nuts', then when someone you know is struggling, they're more likely to feel able to speak up. You can help contribute towards creating this kind of safe environment, whether as a friend, a leader or a colleague. Then it's just a matter of paying attention to people and noticing if someone is acting differently to normal.

There is always this notion that you will make things worse if you explore certain subjects or ask certain questions, but actually, talking about difficult topics and letting people say their biggest worry out loud can really help them process what they are feeling.

The more you have these kinds of conversations, the easier they become: there's no right answer, and you don't need a script. Just focus on the human factor. The subject matter may be a bit unusual or a bit uncomfortable, but ultimately, this is just a chat with someone. Just you, talking to another person.

Jin was Chair of Trustees at Central London Samaritans and has been a listening volunteer for 10 years.

Listening Diary

Keep a listening diary for a week. Record how many times you listened really well. Note down what challenges and distractions you experienced, and what you think went well. Aim to learn at least one new thing about the person who is talking to you and note it down.

Mon ....
....
....

Tues ....
....
....

Wed ....
....
....

Thu ....
....
....

Fri ....
....
....

Sat ....
....
....

Sun ....
....
....
....

Being honest about how we're feeling helps others to open up, too

Hope Virgo suffered with anorexia throughout her teens, before being admitted to the mental health unit of a hospital for a year. She now uses her experiences of mental illness to champion the rights of others, inspire them to get well, and help break the stigma of mental illness.

Having close friends and family to check in with and listen has been really important in Hope's journey. When she was unwell, people knew that she was struggling because she was underweight. Since coming out of hospital, she's had to be more vocal about how she's feeling. She says: 'I have to feel like I'm being listened to, because if I'm not, then my brain automatically switches to: "Right, this is how you can show people you're not OK."'

When Hope was first discharged from hospital, she realised how unprepared she was to go out into the world and deal with day-to-day situations. One of the things she voices in her campaigning work is how important it is to go back to your

GP and ask for help, even if you get turned away. 'When you leave treatment, you're expected to just go out and have as normal a life as you can. But you're not totally prepared with the skills or coping mechanisms to go into various situations. I had to try and learn to navigate those situations on my own – whether that was going travelling, or heading to uni – and find a way to stay in recovery in all these stages of my life. There is nothing wrong with going back and asking for help until you get the support you need.'

Almost 10 years on from her hospital stay, Hope suffered a relapse after the death of her grandmother. What followed was a couple of months of really struggling mentally, and her old coping mechanism of restricting food and over-exercising began again. 'I tried to get support but wasn't able to, because I wasn't underweight. I had this four-week period where I just felt awful all the time. I'd get up in the morning and go to the gym, then cry my whole journey into work, but put on my make-up, say "Everything's fine," and wear a brave face all day. Then I'd get on the tube in the evening to go back home and just cry that entire journey again. I'd get home and be so emotionally, physically and completely exhausted. About three weeks after I'd been turned away, I came very close to ending my life. One of the reasons I didn't was because my little sister rang me at just the right moment, and I had this realisation that if I did end my life, then she would fail her exams and it'd be my fault. So I went back to my GP the following week and got a prescription for antidepressants.'

The medication really helped Hope, but she was wary of telling people other than her close family and friends for fear of judgement. 'The medication gave me energy to just get through the days and clear my head. It helped me to get back on track. I only told my boyfriend and my mum to begin with, then I gradually began to tell a couple of other friends.

I think the main thing for me was getting over feeling guilty that I had to take it, and I was also really worried about it changing me as a person. But we all just need to start doing what's best for ourselves and not stressing about what everyone else is thinking.'

Hope found that when she opened up, the people she was honest with would then start to share as well. 'For me, something that's really helped since going on medication is trying to be a little bit more vulnerable with my friends. It was actually quite a hard thing to learn how to do. I still find it hard. But when my friends message me now and ask how I am, I always try and be really honest. Showing that vulnerability gives others the space to open up as well. It means that, in our friendship group, conversations around mental health are really normal now.'

One of the other things Hope did when she wanted to reach out to others was to send a message to let people know how she was feeling, but also reassure them she was dealing with it responsibly, as opposed to asking them to help her. 'When I had just come out of hospital and was at university, I would message my mum and just say "I'm not feeling OK today," or "I'm struggling a bit." It allowed me to share enough with her so that I didn't have to show my distress through not eating, but it also didn't give her the space to try and fix it because I wasn't giving her too much information: one of my pet hates is people trying to fix me or people feeling sorry for me.'

Sometimes, when you're struggling mentally, you don't want to always talk about your feelings and your emotions. But don't be afraid of being direct and asking questions about what's going on. 'It won't trigger someone to start doing something, if you just say it out loud. When I relapsed, I went for a walk along the South Bank with my best friend, and she just said, very directly: "Are you counting your calories again?" Her being so straightforward really helped, because I was able to say, "Well, yeah, I am, but I'm getting help." It was reassuring for me and for her, and having that to-the-point conversation was helpful. With eating disorders, they're so wrapped up in shame. But by having a direct question like that, it took away the embarrassment associated with it.'

When Hope feels as if she's not being heard, she backs away from opening up and starts to struggle with rumination. This is when you get stuck on certain thoughts that play over and over in your head. 'If I voice it and share those thoughts, even though no one can solve that kind of rumination, it just helps. If I don't talk and if I keep things to myself, I start to think about food again, because I start to feel myself thinking that I need to show people I'm struggling. I need people to see that I don't feel great. So bad feelings manifest in behaviours like restricting or calorie-counting. Then I might start thinking, "I should just give up now and end my life," and it can escalate into a pattern of negative thinking.

'Sometimes wanting to talk to someone is about just having a normal chat, or needing to vent. Conversations about mental health can feel awkward and uncomfortable sometimes, but it feels so amazing when someone takes the time to just be there and listen. It's such a simple thing to do, and anyone can do it. But quite often, we forget to.'

Hope's advice on opening up:

- Listening is important, because it gives people the chance to feel heard and valued and deserving of support.

- It's probably going to feel awkward if someone's telling you a lot of personal stuff. But just let it be OK.

- At the end of the conversation, ask the person: 'Is there anything that I can do to support you with this?' It gives that individual the ownership to share if there is something more they need from you, and it also gives them the space to say, 'No, I just wanted to talk about it,' or, 'Actually, I think I need further help.'

- Self-care is really important. It can be big things like therapy, or little things like listening to music. You have to be really disciplined with it. I know if I don't do it, I'll completely burn out.

- Sometimes, it's just about being there to distract someone. If I'm feeling really rubbish, I might ring up my sister and say, 'Can you just talk at me?' And she will just talk about the most boring stuff ever and I'll listen and it will take my mind off things.

'Listening is not a reaction;
it is a connection.'

Ursula K. Le Guin

Chapter 2:
Loneliness and togetherness

Humans crave attention. We thrive in groups. We are social animals and need other people around us. Feeling connected to others is a basic human need that is essential to our wellbeing. There is a wealth of evidence to show that social connections, whether with a partner, family, friends or work colleagues, can promote good health. Conversely, when we are isolated from others, we can become very unhappy; a lack of supportive relationships or simply a belief that there's no one to turn to can lead to loneliness and, for some, extreme unhappiness and depression.

Loneliness can be in the mind rather than a physical thing. When we talk about loneliness and isolation, we're not talking about living on a farm in the Outer Hebrides. You can be very lonely in a relationship if you feel disconnected, or when you're not getting any validation from anybody else. You can feel alone when you're in the middle of a crowd. You might feel lonely when you look at social media. That feeling of disconnectedness – I don't belong, I don't relate, nobody really gets me – can be exacerbated by digital networks, as the lives we see presented there are often not real and are viewed – quite literally – through a filter. Technology has given us endless possibilities, but we still need human connection to create meaningful relationships. Social media connections add huge value to our lives, but they can't replace the real thing.

The support we receive and give makes us more resilient when bad times come along, and that needs to be nurtured. Listening can really enhance the notion of togetherness. A meaningful interaction between two people can result in authentic moments where we feel heard, recognised, understood and validated.

Human connection and the benefits we get from it can help make us more resilient when there is a crisis, as well as being a safety net for us when we face difficulties. Just being with someone in hard times can be a great support for that person. Our connection with other people – and theirs with us – makes us stronger. When the chips are down, we want to have people around us who care, in whom we can confide and from whom we can get help.

We gain empathy by learning about other people and their problems, and when life takes a difficult turn, we know it makes sense to reach out for help. People need people: they will never stop needing them. Listening and giving each other time is one thing we can resolve to do that will make a big difference.

Give someone your full attention to create a connection

If you take the time to show a friend or family member that you're thinking about them, it's very validating for that person. They might realise that you wouldn't be thinking of them or reaching out unless you thought they were worth it. But our brains think much more quickly than the speed at which we listen, and that means we are often too distracted to listen with our full potential. If you're with somebody who's trying to talk to you and you're looking at your phone, or thinking about what you're going to say next, that stops the other person from talking openly, because they know you're not really focusing on them. When you're speaking to someone in person, you can show you are listening by making a connection through eye contact and not being distracted by your phone bleeping. You need to concentrate on what someone is saying and act appropriately. Time is the most valuable thing you can give people, particularly in a very busy world where there are plenty of constant distractions.

Listening is not a passive thing. It's very active. You're not just taking in what someone is saying; you're processing it, too. It's about making an emotional connection with someone, then responding in a way that gives them time to think and maybe come up with new options. We use silence a lot at Samaritans. Allow silences to happen, and see them as thinking time. If you speak too soon, you run the risk of interrupting someone who has been formulating what they want to say – and it's probably a lot harder for them to say it than it is for us to hear it.

If you ask someone a question and they give a very short answer, you can leave a bit of space, and then say, 'Can you tell me a bit more about that?' Giving people the ability to explore without jumping in is key. Just try to get them to elaborate a little, which makes them think things through in more detail. In a way, it's just about helping people keep talking until they've worked it out, and staying connected with them while they consider their options.

I think people are sometimes frightened to approach somebody who looks as if they're distressed. They're scared to say anything to them, because they don't know how they're going to react if they hear an answer they can't cope with. It feels like a risky thing to do. But whether it's your family, friends or a stranger in the street, it is simply about being a bit kinder, and giving someone some time – and your full attention. That is what allows a connection to be made.

Jenni has been a Samaritans volunteer for 37 years and was previously Chair of Trustees.

There is no wrong or right when listening to someone

The harmony and tension of listening is not an exact science. It's unlikely that you'll achieve a perfect yin-yang balance of conversational art. But don't be afraid of asking someone how they are feeling. Quite often, we can feel nervous when reaching out to people we know – friends, family, a loved one or a colleague – because we think we're not equipped with the right skills to help them. Perhaps we think it might be a burden to take on someone's baggage, especially if we've got issues of our own.

It doesn't matter what you say

Sometimes it's difficult to know how to start a tricky conversation. We can feel scared of approaching someone to ask how they are feeling because we are nervous of saying the wrong thing or reacting in an unhelpful way. But try not to be afraid of getting it wrong. You don't need to be a trained mental health professional, a counsellor or a therapist

'I've learned that people will forget what you said, people will forget what you did, but people will never forget how you made them feel.'

Maya Angelou

to help someone who's having a tough time. You can help by learning more about mental health and educating yourself about the problems we might all face at some point in our lives, and how they might manifest. You can equip yourself with the basic tools of active listening, and treat others with compassion and empathy in order to connect with them and be there for them. You can be confident that standing (or sitting, or walking) alongside the person you are trying to help, and simply saying, 'OK, let's sit with this problem, together,' can make a huge difference in people's lives.

Imagine a friend telling you they have been feeling depressed for a while, and they are not sure what to do about it. You might feel shocked or surprised – perhaps you thought you would have spotted the signs, or maybe this friend had seemed fine, always making jokes and messing about to entertain you and your other friends. You might feel lost for words. Don't worry: this is totally natural. It's perfectly OK to just say: 'I'm sorry, I don't know what to say,' or, 'That sounds awful for you; I had no idea that's how you were feeling.' Instead of responding right away and stumbling over your words, or saying something you haven't thought through, you could say something like: 'I'm so sorry, I didn't know you were feeling this way. I think I need a few minutes to take this in as I don't really know what to say right now, but I want to be there for you.'

People will always remember how they felt in a good conversation where they have been listened to, even if they don't remember everything that is said. People phone Samaritans in all kinds of states of distress, from anxious and upset to desperate. They might cry or shout until they have everything out of their system. In those moments, they won't remember the details of the call, but they will remember how it made them feel. Often, people describe feeling safe, as if they were being held in the moment, or as if a huge weight had been lifted off their shoulders.

After an intense and emotional conversation, don't panic if you feel like it didn't go as well as you had hoped. There is no perfect way to handle a difficult talk. If you have shown compassion and made sure the person knows they are not alone and how to access further support, you will already have made a real difference. If, after your conversation, you get the feeling that someone is still feeling low, you might want to suggest that they get some extra help, whether that's talking to someone like a counsellor or seeking specific advice for their situation.

You could try saying:

• 'Have you talked to anyone else about this?'

• 'Would you like to get some help?'

• 'Would you like me to help you look into the kind of support that's available?'

• 'Would you like me to come with you?'

For someone who seems reluctant to seek further help, you could maybe say, 'Do you have someone you trust who you can go to?' or, 'If it helps, you can talk to me, any time.'

Just remember, you can't pressure anyone into getting help – they need to be ready. The person you're trying to help might not want anything formal like a counsellor. They might want to try medication, or they might be interested in peer support groups where they can share experiences with others who have been in the same position. Often, talking to other people can feel more comfortable than going to a professional.

You can't force someone to open up. But by letting them know you are there to listen, you might alter their state of mind enough for them to feel able to open up in a day or two, whether to you or someone else.

> 'Every session attended by the analyst must have no history and no future. What is "known" about the patient is of no further consequence: it is either false or irrelevant... The only point of importance in any session is the unknown.'
>
> Wilfred Bion

Don't worry if you say something wrong

The psychoanalyst Wilfred Bion wrote about approaching each session with a patient without memory and without desire. It reminds me of how we listen as Samaritans – we kind of forget everything about the person we are talking to. We have no agenda: our only motivation is to be there, in that particular moment, listening intently.

The best and most helpful conversations are the ones when people say, 'What does that mean for you? Tell me what your experiences are. What is that like for you? How does that feel for you? What does that do for you?' Even when a situation feels unfamiliar to you, you can ask these questions and then clarify what you've heard. Not only will this help you understand better, it's likely that it will be just as helpful for the person you're listening to.

In our everyday lives, it is important for us to initiate these sorts of conversations if we notice that someone is acting differently or appears to be upset. It's no more than making an observation or expressing a concern. Sure, sometimes it can feel a bit awkward, probably because we don't want to make things worse or say the wrong thing. But saying: 'I'm here to listen, if you'd like to talk,' is enough to show you care. And you do have to care, because genuine concern makes a real difference. It's essential. Grasp the nettle. Even if you are wrong and that person doesn't want to talk, you've not lost anything by asking.

When I take a call at Samaritans, I'm never worried that I might say the wrong thing. And that's not because I'm horribly conceited and arrogant: it is because I know that I probably will say the wrong thing at some point. There isn't really a right thing to say – but if I worried about saying the wrong thing all the time, I'd never say anything. We're human and we're fallible. We make mistakes. But the key is to have the humility to roll back when we've made a mistake and say, 'I'm so sorry. I've misunderstood what you meant. Let's start this conversation again,' or, 'It feels like I said something that has upset you. And that was the last thing I wanted to do. I've made a mistake. I'm sorry. Can we start again with it?' I genuinely feel if we listen with an open heart and an open mind, then actually, we are not going to get it wrong. Sincerity is everything.

For Samaritans volunteers, empathy should be a given. But courage is also key. I would encourage everybody to be brave when they see somebody who's upset – go and ask if they are OK. It's easy to say nothing, or simply sweep it under the carpet and think it's going to get better. It's really easy to let ourselves off the hook by thinking, Well, I don't want to make the situation worse.

The only way you could make it worse is to talk about yourself too much, rather than letting your friend, or partner, or whoever it is, say what they need to. If a friend tells you they've split up with a boyfriend or girlfriend, your natural instinct may be to tell them about a similar situation that you went through. While that person may appreciate where you're coming from in your desire to get alongside them and make them feel less alone, it's important to remember that our experience and their experience, despite superficial similarities, is going to be entirely different. So, you can't let the conversation become about you and your experiences, rather than about them and what they're going through. At Samaritans, we don't tell callers about our personal experiences, even if they ask, because how would it help them in their situation? In conversations with friends, it's more likely you will bring your own experiences to the table. But just remember to let the other person say everything that they need to say about their situation.

It might be that someone needs a bit of a nudge to open up. Sometimes there has to be some reciprocity. And that's good, as long as we know why we're doing it and what our motivations are. We do get somewhere with people by sharing, and showing you've got common ground – being open or allowing yourself to be vulnerable – can help someone recognise they are in a safe space in which they can open up.

Often, the wisest thing I ever do on a call is shut up. This allows that silence to be filled by the other person, who fills in the blanks themselves in a way that speaks to them. I don't need to say 'Do this, try that, I found this helpful,' because, invariably, they don't care. What's important is for that person to find their own way forwards: we're just providing a structure. There's no great wisdom there. It's just about knowing to be quiet at the right time.

Be careful not to predict how the person you're listening to might think or react. Even if you know someone well, you might not realise how they are actually feeling. Listen to them with an open mind. There are all sorts of situations, such as grief, redundancy, abuse or being a victim of crime, that can cause people to react in different or surprising ways. Some people will go through something really huge in their lives and not bat an eyelid. Then something seemingly insignificant goes wrong, and that suddenly feels like the end of the world for them. But whether it's a major life event or just a bad day, listening is about sharing a common humanity with someone, and working out if I am able to support them, to listen to them, and to take their upset seriously, so that they have the time and space to work out what's actually going on in a way that makes sense to them.

Matt, Samaritans branch director

We are all human

Kindness is hugely underrated and yet it is a way of showing understanding of another person's needs, which in turn is comforting and practical. It shows empathy and humanity, community and belonging: all of it so important for our mental health.

Kindness towards ourselves is equally as important. In this competitive rat race of a world, we need to give ourselves a break, be forgiving of ourselves and know that, whatever, we are good enough.

Mistakes are vital in order to learn. I often feel anxious when I've made some kind of mistake or misjudgement. My way of dealing with it is to face up to it and take responsibility for it, and then to sit down and forgive myself for simply being human!

Julie Walters, Samaritans Ambassador

Chapter 3:
Understanding stress

As humans, we all have mental health, just as we all have physical health. The only difference is that you can't see it. Which is maybe what makes it harder to talk about – if you have a plaster cast on your arm or leg, you will elicit sympathy from those you know and probably be asked questions like 'Does it hurt?' and 'How long will it take to heal?' But – short of putting a bandage on your head that reads 'My brain isn't feeling so good today' – the only way to let someone know your mental wellbeing is suffering is to tell them. And there are so many misconceptions about mental health out there, it's no wonder people feel nervous about speaking out.

Each one of us has a range that we move up and down at different points in our lives, going from being mentally well at one end to mentally unwell or troubled at the other. Some people might have mental health conditions or diagnosed illnesses such as OCD, bipolar or schizophrenia, that make them more likely to be at the very distressed or troubled end of the spectrum for more of the time. Other people might have experienced an incident or adverse life event that pushes them to the mentally unwell end of the scale, where they experience worry, low mood or insomnia. Some people may feel lonely and isolated; others may be anxious or stressed. We all need to recognise the feelings and emotions that are part of that range, and we must be prepared to have a conversation about where we – and those around us – are at any point along that spectrum, in order to try and avoid escalation into more intense distress.

Fight or flight

It can also be really helpful to understand the neuroscience behind the listening process and why verbalising emotions can help. Because actually, it's quite a biological thing. In terms of neurology, the emotional bit of the brain is quite primitive. But our fight-or-flight response mechanism, which deals with the perception of danger, can have a very real effect on us, physically as well as emotionally.

It begins in the amygdala – a small, almond-shaped region in the middle of your brain that's responsible for decision-making, emotional reactions and memory. In the face of a perceived threat, the amygdala fires up a response that triggers your nervous system. Basically, you get flooded with adrenaline, which makes you stronger and faster and helps you escape.

The physical sensation that accompanies this rush of hormones is an increase in blood pressure. Your heart begins to beat faster to get oxygen and sugar to your muscles, sweating increases as the blood flow changes and your lungs work harder as you breathe. Your stomach and guts churn, blood vessels dilate and muscles tense. You might shake, turn pale or flushed, and get a dry mouth.

'Fight or flight' was a necessary function for our ancestors, who needed an extra boost of strength when hunting or fleeing from a predator. In some situations today it is still necessary for us to use strength in the face of challenge or adversity: athletes about to run a race, or firefighters as they enter a burning building, for example. But what if you're not a gladiator? Or a boxer? Or rescuing someone who's fallen in a river? This same stress response can occur in reaction to an emotional problem instead of a physical one – and when it does, our bodies react in the same way.

In the short term, the stress response can be helpful if something bad happens and we need to run on emergency fumes. When we're facing a crisis, it can help us power through: it can be what helps us get up each day, enables us to put one foot in front of the other, and do all the things we need to. This is unfeasible for the long term, though, and when the adrenaline from a fight-or-flight situation dissipates, we are suddenly exhausted, and our energy crashes.

Most of the time, we self-regulate. But sometimes, a stress-response episode can reoccur. Like a fuse that keeps tripping the wrong way, the response can be harder to switch off, and can result in anxiety, fear, depression or aggression. Our perception can become skewed – we might feel like we're totally out of control, or we might battle for extreme control to try and alter the situation. Repeat episodes of these kinds of feelings – this combination of emotional reaction and physical response – are known as panic attacks.

The act of speech forms a very important function in managing our wellbeing. It enables us to label emotions, articulate them and, in doing so, process thoughts from the feeling to the thinking part of the brain. Once the thinking part of the brain is back in action, we start to find some solutions because we're not so overwhelmed. This is one of the reasons why the Samaritans listening model works so well: by listening, we allow the other person to speak, helping them to rationalise and form their own conclusions.

How the brain is affected by stress

UKCP Psychotherapist Dr Dwight Turner

When we are stressed, it affects our brain chemistry. Stress hormones – cortisol and adrenaline – release into our bodies and minds from the amygdala. The same stress response is triggered whether the catalyst is a big bear or an overdue bill. If we don't release our stress hormones, they build up and make us unwell, because prolonged stress over a period of time affects the way our minds work.

Stress also affects our brain function. The surge of stress hormones from the amygdala temporarily shuts down the prefrontal cortex of the brain (the cognitive thinking part of the mind), and neural activity focuses around the amygdala and the primal part of the brain, pushing us literally into survival mode. This can give us an extra burst of energy, but can also stop us from thinking clearly.

As the primal brain engages, we begin to think less rationally: our body focuses on our survival through fight or flight, and the brain's reasoning and language structures stop engaging. A sustained period of stress without any release through relaxation and exercise can be life-threatening. Long-term stress maintains this temporary shrinking of the prefrontal cortex and increases the size of the amygdala, which then also reduces the size of other parts of the brain involved in rational thought and planning. Chronic stress over a period of time affects brain size, function and structure, and even your genetics.

Liken this to the brain's capacity for learning: if you play guitar for eight hours a day, then the parts of the brain responsible for helping you play the guitar will get larger. If you think stressful thoughts for eight hours a day, then those parts of the brain are going to get larger.

When your brain detects a stressful situation, it releases cortisol, which primes your body for action. As levels of cortisol rise, electrical signals in the hippocampus (the emotional part of the brain associated with reasoning, memories and stress control) deteriorate. Therefore, when the hippocampus weakens, so does your ability to control stress. Prolonged stress also results in fewer new brain cells being made in the hippocampus, which makes it harder to learn and remember things, setting the stage for more serious problems like depression and Alzheimer's disease.

The good news is that simple activities like exercise, rest and meditation can reduce the cortisol in your body and help to reverse these stress impacts.

Relaxation technique

Box breathing

It might sound simple, but controlled breathing can be a useful tool for feeling calmer quickly and reducing feelings of stress and anxiety.

This technique is easy to memorise, and can be done almost anywhere. Practise it for as long as you need to, and share the technique with those you feel might appreciate it.

All you need to do is this:

1. Breathe in for four seconds.
2. Hold your breath for four seconds.
3. Breathe out for four seconds.
4. Wait four seconds before breathing in again.

Keep repeating this until you start to feel calmer. Look for both mental and physical signs, like your thoughts and your heartbeat slowing down.

People with anxiety or those who suffer from stress may already know what triggers their negative thoughts and feelings. This breathing exercise can help someone if they know they are about to encounter a certain trigger, or immediately after they have done.

Muscle relaxation exercise

This technique will teach you how to practise progressive muscle relaxation. Some people find this helps them to feel calmer. It can take around five minutes, but you can practise for any length of time.

Progressive muscle relaxation involves tensing and releasing pairs of muscles in sequence. It can help if you imagine tension leaving your body as you release your muscles. You'll need a quiet, private space for this to work well. You might like to read through the steps of this simple technique before you start.

- Find somewhere to sit, with your feet planted flat on the ground, shoulder-width apart. If you prefer, you can lie down instead.

- Take a deep breath in through your nose, hold it for a few seconds, and then breathe out slowly through your mouth.

- Try to keep your attention focused on your body. Notice any physical sensations you're feeling. Keep breathing all the way in and out slowly and steadily.

- If you notice your mind wandering, acknowledge it, then gently bring your focus back to your body.

- Start with the muscles in your head. Tense your forehead muscles by raising your eyebrows and holding for up to 10 seconds. Breathe in as you tense these muscles.

- Now release, imagining tension leaving your body as you breathe out.

- Rest for a few seconds before moving on to the next group of muscles, working down throughout your body. Start with the other muscles in your face, before moving down to your neck and shoulders. Then move on to your arms, then your chest, your stomach, your legs and your feet.

- When you've finished, don't get up straight away. Stay where you are for a minute or so. Then, when you do get up, do so slowly.

You can practise this technique whenever you notice yourself becoming stressed or anxious, and you can share it with others who you think might be finding it hard to relax.

Don't be afraid to ask for help

Sophie, 23, began experiencing anxiety at around the age of seven. At secondary school she struggled to find her identity amid the pressures of work, fitting in and friendship groups, once describing a moment when, despite being within a big group of friends in class, she felt completely alone. That feeling of isolation set off a wave of anxiety which seemed to grow as she went on to university. Sophie realised what she was feeling wasn't right and so, in the summer of her first year, she opened up to two friends about what she was experiencing. 'I felt like it was the right time. I needed support and we were all on holiday together. I knew they couldn't run off. They just said "It's fine. When we get back, we can go to the doctor and sort it out."'

But when she got home from university for the summer holidays, things felt a lot harder. Sophie got to the point where she would wake up every day feeling like there was no way she'd be able to get through the next two years of university. She felt as if her negative thoughts and feelings were paralysing her. She didn't know how to tell her parents, fearing that they would worry about her and that she would be burdening them. Eventually, she sent them a text message that said, 'I'm struggling. I think I need help.'

By the time they came home from work that day, her parents had had time to prepare themselves for an emotional conversation, so they were able to be composed. They thanked Sophie for letting them know how she was feeling and were supportive. They helped her book a doctor's appointment, and offered to go with her, but accepted that she would rather go with a friend.

Before going to see the doctor, Sophie wrote down a long list of everything she had been thinking and feeling, because she couldn't deal with the pressure of talking through it all. She was diagnosed with anxiety and depression, but was left feeling uncertain about what to do next. 'It felt like a kind of shut-down after the diagnosis. I was just left to my own devices and told to read up about it and speak to someone if I could. But I wasn't put on a waiting list for counselling. I was just given a leaflet, and that was it.'

Unfortunately, Sophie's stress and anxiety increased over the next two years at university, exacerbated by a bad relationship with someone who lowered her sense of self-worth. She found herself in a cycle of anxiety, panic attacks and negative thoughts. The breakup of the relationship coincided with the summer holidays, where she was at home alone a lot of the time. 'I felt completely worthless, like there was no point because I couldn't even stand up and do a presentation in class. I wondered how I would ever get a job after uni.'

Sophie's anxiety escalated to the point where she would wake up with a feeling of dread, as if something awful had happened, and this would remain a constant throughout her day. 'I lived with this fear that something would go wrong, or that something bad was going to happen. I had this continual worry that I had done or said something wrong.'

'My heart would race, I would sweat, I would shake and I had this feeling like I couldn't breathe in air. Emotionally it felt like I was in a dark, deep hole and there was no ladder to get out – or even if there was a ladder, it was halfway down and I couldn't quite reach it. I would wake up and think, how am I going to get through the next 12 hours? Some days I couldn't face it; I would just stay in bed.'

Sophie went back to the doctor and was put on the waiting list for CBT (cognitive behavioural therapy). The waiting list was around seven months. During that time, she felt like she needed more immediate support. 'I remember one day, waking with anxiety and wondering how to get through the day. I wasn't suicidal, but I knew I couldn't keep living like that. I couldn't cope with how bad it felt. I couldn't keep waking up in fear and having that feeling of panic just stay with me until I went to bed again at night. I just couldn't see how to live with that level of anxiety. I called my parents, who were at work, and they gave me a list of how to structure my day – watch some TV, go for a walk, do something to focus my mind.'

But Sophie found herself at home alone, in a really dark place, with her self-doubt and lack of confidence in overdrive. 'I didn't know what to do with myself. I felt like I had no way out. I had this feeling of desperation – I just wanted to get it all off my chest.' And so she called Samaritans. 'They never said, "You should do this, you should do that." They asked me, "How do you think you are going to get through this? How are you going to help yourself?" It gave me the tools to process my thoughts myself and get through it myself.

'I was on the phone to them for about an hour, just speaking through everything that had happened. Having someone there to listen was exactly what I needed. It literally felt like a weight had been lifted off my shoulders after speaking to them. The person seemed to understand the way I felt and they reminded me that there were things that I could do to help me get through it. Just having someone to speak to was so helpful. I felt like

I could be completely honest and admit that I didn't know how to get through the day. They didn't give me any advice – they just listened. And that made me feel less alone.'

Sophie's tips on asking for help with anxiety

• Prepare. Write a list for your doctor outlining how you feel so you know what you want to say. Writing a list always helps for me: I also write lists to help me work out a structure for my day, even if the only things I write down are having a shower, watching TV, coming off social media or going for a walk at a certain time.

• Send a text message to let someone know that you want to talk to them – it gives them a bit of time to prepare and for both of you to build up a bit of resilience before the conversation.

• Be transparent about what you need. Tell someone that you just want to talk to them and want to feel like they are there for you, but that they don't have to help you immediately, or at all. It's the sharing that's the most important bit. I never wanted anyone to say: 'Why don't you change universities or get a job?' I just wanted them to support me, not judge the choices I was making.

• Just letting someone know what's going on can be reassuring, because if you then say, 'I'm not feeling that great today,' you know that they already know what you're talking about without it feeling awkward. And knowing that people understand and accept what you're going through makes everything easier and makes you feel more supported. I know now that my friends and family are there for me, and that if I really need help, I can go to them and ask for it.

Chapter 4:
How to tell if someone needs to talk

We all have good days and bad days: it's part of being human. Sometimes, we might simply wake up on the wrong side of the bed, have a bit of a grump, or feel worn down and jaded by our day-to-day work pressures, social engagements, quarrels with friends or family trivialities. At different times in our lives, we will all probably traverse different parts of the pathway of psychological wellbeing, moving up and down the mental health spectrum from 'flourishing' – a phrase coined by American psychologist Corey Keyes – to 'moderate' and then 'languishing' mental health, which usually describes a diagnosable mental illness.

It's likely that either you, or someone you know, has been through an experience where day-to-day troubles seem to snowball. What might be a seemingly minor issue on another day suddenly feels insurmountable. Or perhaps there is a build-up of pressure around numerous contributing factors: an argument with a friend alongside a conflict at work; money pressures alongside a strained conversation with a family member. Perhaps three or four negative events might all happen at once, and things you would be able to handle as stand-alone incidents suddenly feel like they are overwhelming, or too difficult to deal with.

So how do you tell if someone else is having a hard time?

At Samaritans, we know that some of the reasons people find life tough and struggle to cope are debt and other financial worries, job loss, work stress, relationship breakdowns, family problems, and feelings of loneliness and isolation. Men, in particular, avoid speaking out when they find life tough and often don't want to burden others with their issues. First, it's important to recognise that you might not always be able to spot the signs that someone is struggling to cope. Emotional distress can be hard to identify: everyone responds to things in their own individual way, and it can be tricky to notice if a partner or a friend is suffering.

Some people eat more, some people eat less; some people seem down, some make jokes to deflect; some people's libidos go up, some lose their libido entirely. You're looking for any significant change in normal behavioural patterns. If somebody who's usually extrovert becomes withdrawn, and vice versa, or if someone stops doing something that they've always enjoyed, then perhaps there's an issue. Usually, you can tell when someone is acting out of character. Go with your gut instinct.

Certain times of the year can magnify feelings of loneliness, for example Christmas time, when it might feel like everyone is excited about getting together with loved ones, buying and exchanging gifts, and grappling with a packed social calendar. But for many people, festive occasions can evoke feelings of anxiety. The demands of yearly events spent alone or under significant stress after someone has passed away – a birthday, anniversary, holiday season or festivity – can lead to high emotions. Things that may ordinarily seem trivial can become contentious and put additional strain on people, so be extra mindful at these times.

Behaviours to look out for

Perhaps you have a friend who hasn't been socialising as much recently. You might be worried that a colleague isn't showing up for work, or you may have noticed that your partner is more tired and withdrawn than usual and doesn't seem to be communicating in the way that you're used to. Don't be afraid to say: 'I hope you don't mind me saying it, but you don't seem yourself at the moment. Are you OK?' Most people will instinctively respond with: 'I'm fine.' But you can follow up, saying: 'OK, well, if you're not, I have time to chat or would like to listen to what you're going through. I'm here for you.'

Signs and behaviours that may indicate someone might be having a tough time could include:

• lacking energy or appearing particularly tired;

• seeming irritable, restless and agitated;

- appearing more tearful than usual;

- not wanting to talk to or be with people;

- not wanting to do things they usually enjoy;

- changing their routines, such as sleeping or eating more or less than normal;

- using alcohol or drugs to cope with feelings;

- finding it hard to cope with everyday things;

- not liking or taking care of themselves, or feeling that they don't matter;

- being untypically clumsy or accident-prone;

- becoming withdrawn or losing touch with friends and family;

- not replying to messages or seeming distant;

- becoming angry, aggressive or defensive; or

- doing more risky things, or becoming self-destructive.

Big life changes

Interpreting how someone else is feeling can be difficult and, for some people, there may not be any obvious changes like the ones listed above. Emotions show up differently in everyone, and they may be more difficult to spot if you're not seeing much of the person you're concerned about. It's important to understand that there are certain situations that can affect how someone is feeling, for example:

• relationship and family problems;

• loss, including the loss of a friend or a family member through bereavement;

• financial worries;

• job-related stress;

• college or study-related stress;

• loneliness and isolation;

• depression;

• painful and/or disabling physical illness.

The list above details examples of significant change, and it's particularly important to look out for those around you who might be experiencing these big shifts in their lives, as they can all trigger new and conflicting emotions. More often than not, these times pass and we pick ourselves up, shake ourselves down and adjust to our new circumstances. Change can bring positive outcomes, such as personal growth and new opportunities. But adjusting to change can be very difficult, and change that's outside our control can make us feel anxious and stressed. For situations like the ones above, we should never underestimate the value of showing concern and care for each other. If you notice someone behaving differently to normal, then take the time to check in and see if they are OK.

Sometimes people say things which might help you recognise that they are struggling to cope. Listen out for negative self-talk, when someone is down on themselves, or talks about feeling hopeless, helpless or worthless. They might mention feeling trapped, as if they are unable to break out of internal thoughts and feelings, or that they have a desire to escape from experiences in the outside world.

They might make leading statements, either verbally, in messages or on social media, such as, 'You wouldn't believe what I've been through,' or 'It's like the whole world is against me.' People sometimes say these things in the hope you will pick up on them and ask what they mean so that they can talk about how they're feeling. Or, they might make negative statements about themselves, such as 'No one loves me,' or 'I'm a waste of space.' Often, they might pretend that they are joking when they say these things.

We all experience not being OK differently. Not everyone who is struggling to cope will use these phrases. In fact, some people might not be chatting as much as they usually would, or may not be posting or messaging at all. If there's someone you're worried about and you want to check in with them and make sure they're OK, try to do this using the channel you normally communicate with them through.

Be mindful of someone's tone

UKCP Psychotherapist Andy Ryan
When listening to someone, be mindful of the tone of voice they use, and their general way of being. If you are seeing a constant low mood, risk-taking behaviour or notice someone withdrawing, this is where interaction may be required. Be aware of and comment on positive changes and ask open questions.

Also, be aware if the person you are listening to becomes numb or increasingly desensitised to events in their life. This can be an indication they need to increase the frequency of appointments or support from their therapist, if they have one, or the support offered by family members and friends.

At work, you might notice someone making a sudden and steady withdrawal from social connection, or notice that they don't want to be asked questions such as 'How are you?' This can be another sign that they're having a hard time or going through something difficult.

Recognising when someone might need help

Elizabeth reached out to Samaritans after a period of intense depression. After a bad car accident, she suffered from severe emotional distress that left her feeling lonely and isolated. She lost a new job because she wasn't able to drive into work, and her thoughts began to spiral out of control. One night, Elizabeth felt so depressed, she even wrote goodbye emails to her loved ones, because although she didn't want to end her life, she couldn't see how to keep going – there was no light at the end of the tunnel.

One of the warning signs for Elizabeth's family and friends that something was wrong was that she had stopped communicating on their group chats. Usually full of jokes and banter, she got quieter and quieter until she wasn't saying anything at all. She would usually go out with friends every couple of weeks, but found herself starting to make excuses or saying no, and when she was with them, she wasn't being her usual outgoing self.

It's not always easy to spot the signs when someone is feeling low, depressed or anxious, and if the person withdraws from their ordinary activities, it can make it even harder. Elizabeth's advice is: 'Make sure you ask someone twice how they're feeling. Just say, "Are you sure you're OK? Do you want to talk about something? I'm here if you need me." We have this very British way of saying "You alright?" But it's just a common courtesy. So sometimes simply following it up with "Are you sure?" can help to open up a conversation.'

A lot of the time, we're just thinking about what we're going to say next, rather than listening to the person who is speaking. 'Everybody's really busy trying to give their own opinions. For me, when I finally got the courage to start talking – whether to a family member or a friend, sometimes it felt like all they wanted to do was throw opinions at me and say, "Why don't you do this? Why don't you do that? Take a break, have a bath, have a cup of tea." And I would think, "Are you actually listening to me? Or are you just telling me what you think?" They would focus on what would be the solution rather than just listening, and that made me retreat into myself.'

Even though she finds it hard to open up, Elizabeth now finds that talking through a problem helps her feel or see things differently because it's nice to get somebody else's perspective. Now, when she talks to a friend and tells them she's feeling a bit anxious, because they know her, they might say, 'Maybe you don't have to worry quite so much about that,' or 'Have you thought about trying this? It helped you before.'

'Sometimes someone might say something that resonates with you, and it can just help you to think a bit differently rather than letting the feeling take over,' Elizabeth says. 'It's good sometimes to have a bit of reassurance, too, to be reminded that I don't need to worry as much. Your friends and family know you better than anyone else and this can be helpful when offering a different point of view. But what I find most helpful is when they ask: "It sounds like what you're saying is… Is that right? Have you thought about maybe…" Rather than just saying, "Here's what I think you should do."'

Elizabeth realises how hard it can be for loved ones to take that first step in starting what might be a tricky conversation. 'Sometimes it can feel hard to reach out to someone who you think might be struggling with their emotions. You might wonder what to say or worry that you're not equipped to deal with what they might say back to you. But just give someone time to open up. If you go in firing questions, it's going to come across as confrontational, so the person might back away or get defensive. If you go for a walk, and have more of a general chat, you'll probably find a natural rhythm where someone feels comfortable to speak to you or open up.'

Another thing that stopped Elizabeth from sharing her feelings when she was experiencing depression was that she didn't want to be a burden. 'I thought that if I went to someone in my family and told them about my problems, they'd worry about me, and that added an extra layer of guilt and responsibility for me. You don't want to be a burden or feel like you are wasting someone's time. You can get into a mindset that you're not worth it. But that's all it is – a mindset.'

When Elizabeth saw a counsellor, they did a lot of outside walking and talking. 'It can be quite intimidating to sit in somebody's office and feel like you're being grilled, but walking next to somebody gives you so much more space to think. Looking back, it would have been nice to go for a walk and have a chat with a friend or family member. Sometimes, it's hard to really be open with someone because when you've got a lot on your mind, you might worry that they're not going to understand you. But I really like being outside, so that would have given me a bit of space, in both senses, to talk.'

The other thing she found was that people were nervous of having frank conversations. 'People couldn't believe it when

I was signed off work. Only a couple of people contacted me, and it turned out that others didn't get in touch because they didn't know what to say. They were nervous. Sometimes it doesn't matter what you say. You can text "Thinking of you" and that can remind somebody that they are important. Or you can just ask, "Are you OK? Hope you're well." People can overthink it and worry but just a small gesture, like sending a short message, can feel like a lifeline.'

Elizabeth now recognises the power in sharing and opening up about her feelings and how positive that can be. 'I know people are worried about judgement, particularly with mental health. But sharing and being kind to others is the only way forwards. It just needs one person to have the courage to start a conversation, and that can create a domino effect. When I was at school, no one talked about mental health, and so it was only from going through stuff myself that I realised other people felt the same way. As soon as I start to talk about my experiences, it helps other people to open up. It's like it gives them the courage to say, "Well if she can do it, maybe I can do it, too." People are good at putting on a brave face, but you don't always need to. It's OK to not be OK.'

Elizabeth's advice for starting a tricky conversation

• Really opening up isn't something most people can do very quickly. It's going to take time. You can't push somebody into talking. I know that if someone tries to force me to open up, I do the opposite and close down. It's almost like a defence mechanism. If you feel attacked, and you feel pressured, then you're just going to go the opposite way. So let the person know you are there for them whenever they feel ready to talk. It might be weeks later that they feel ready.

- Focus on the person you're listening to. Remember that a good listener is somebody that engages with the speaker and makes them feel heard, through eye contact and positive body language, like nodding and avoiding crossing your arms and legs.

- Don't tell someone to 'Just cheer up' – it can make them feel 10 times worse. It totally invalidates the strength of their feelings. It can be tempting to say things like 'it could be worse', just because you don't know what else to say, but it can really make the person you're listening to feel worthless.

- Try going outside to walk and talk. Then all you have to do is ask questions and be interested in the answers. Giving someone the time and space to talk is the most important thing.

It's always best to check in

We live in a world where saying 'I'm fine' when asked how you are is an expected response, and this can make it harder to actually admit when there might be something more going on, or when we're feeling miserable and might need to talk. Often, you can just pick up on a feeling that something's not quite right with someone. In those instances, I think it's always best to send a little message, just saying 'Are you OK?' It can be difficult to tell that something's wrong if somebody has retreated a little bit from their normal daily routines, for example, not coming to their usual pub quiz, or an exercise class. If someone is staying at home and not wanting to go out much, it can indicate that they are struggling – but it also means that it can be harder to know what's going on with them.

Often people will feel nervous about asking if someone is OK, and might think that it's none of their business, or that they don't want to intrude. But it's always best to check in – and it's likely that the person will be grateful to know you are there for them, whether they want to talk or not. It could be as simple as dropping a text saying, 'Hey, I really miss not seeing you,' or, 'Just checking that you're OK. No pressure to reply – just thought I'd ask,' or. 'I just saw your tweet, you OK?'

Sometimes it can be as simple as going into the kitchen area to make a cup of tea at the same time as someone else and just saying, 'Hey, how are things? I haven't seen you for ages.' They might not respond straight away, but a conversation opener can be helpful to let someone know you care and are there for them.

If I do send someone a message to check in, I'll always make sure to add 'no pressure to reply'. Sometimes it can be hard for people to respond to messages when they're feeling low – or they might feel like they need to put on a front and say they are fine. It's good to give them a choice as to whether they respond or not. Reassuring someone that they don't have to do anything, or say anything, and that there's no expectation, is a good idea.

Reaching out and making that connection can feel like a lifeline to someone.

Concetta, Samaritans listening volunteer

When someone might need further help

UKCP Psychotherapist Dr Christian Buckland

There are a number of clues that can help us make a decision about whether to help a friend seek additional support.

Verbal warning signs might include statements such as:

- 'I can't take it anymore.'
- 'Nobody cares about me.'
- 'I can't see the point anymore.'
- 'It will never get any better.'
- 'Everyone would be better off if I weren't here.'
- 'Nothing matters anymore.'
- 'I'm going to kill myself.'

They might mention significant changes in feelings, such as:

- loneliness
- anger
- hopelessness
- overwhelming guilt
- desperation
- worthlessness
- isolation
- sadness

You or they might have noticed significant changes in their actions and behaviours, including:

- increased crying
- emotional outbursts
- deliberate self-harm
- increased risk-taking
- withdrawing or isolating
- putting their affairs in order
- talking about their will
- giving away items and possessions
- significant behavioural changes
- increased alcohol or drug use
- significant changes in their relationship with food

Where to direct someone to seek further help

It can be extremely difficult to know the most appropriate place to signpost a friend to. If you feel someone is in crisis and requires immediate attention, then the safest option is to call emergency services on 999, or to attend your local A&E department at hospital. If the friend does not require immediate attention, but you feel they do need help soon, then suggest they speak to their GP or call NHS 111, as they will be able to conduct an assessment of your friend's current situation and make any necessary referrals either through local NHS services or privately, if this is an option.

Some people find it very difficult to talk to their GP, particularly when the topic is sensitive. If they need more time and space, then a psychotherapist can really help. It is sometimes possible to get referred to a psychotherapist within the NHS through a GP, although sadly access to this in-depth support is inconsistent across the UK, and there are often waiting lists for appointments. Encourage your friend to talk to their GP about their options and to consider how talking therapies could be an important part of their support and recovery.

Recommending Samaritans is also an incredibly helpful option. Samaritans listening support can be used in conjunction with other services or on its own, so it is always a good option to recommend to a friend. Call 116 123 or email jo@samaritans.org. See pages 187–92 for a full list of resources and organisations.

PART TWO

How to be a Better Listener

'Courage is what it
takes to stand up and speak;
courage is also what it takes
to sit down and listen.'

Winston Churchill

Chapter 5:
How to start a tricky conversation

Getting started

It takes courage

There is no right or wrong way to begin a conversation that you suspect might be difficult, deep, or even distressing. Whether someone has been affected by grief, has been declared bankrupt, is having difficulty being more open about their sexuality or has just announced a divorce, the most important thing is to show up for them – to check in and show that you care. You might take some food over to their place or just pop by to check that they're managing OK. Sometimes people don't want to be asked 'Are you alright?' all the time, and while some may appreciate being asked how they're feeling directly, others may need a gentler approach. So ask the person how you can best support them. Simply letting someone know that you're there for them when they are ready to open up is a great first step – just being available, or present, can be enough.

But the next step can feel tricky. You might fret about whether or not you have the right knowledge to help your friend through what they are experiencing. You might be afraid that their words will remind you of a bad experience you've had (see page 179 for more advice on this issue). You might worry that once you invite them to open up, their tears could be like a tap that you won't be able to turn off, and you won't know what to do next. All of these concerns are perfectly natural. Whether you are an introvert, an extrovert, an over-thinker or a fixer, there is no right or wrong way to offer – or accept – help, and there's no right or wrong way to react and respond in the moment. But if we're equipped with the right tools for how to spot that someone might really need to talk, and be listened to, then at least we can give it our best shot.

There are endless possible outcomes when you talk to somebody, and either party might experience confusion or frustration. But it can also end in greater understanding or clarity. Whatever the outcome, there is almost always some kind of change, however big or small.

Ask 'Are you sure?'

Sometimes you can try digging a little deeper when someone's words don't quite match up with how they are acting. 'Are you sure?' can be a powerful question. It can be the sign someone needs that it is OK to be honest. When asked how they are, everyone has, at some point in their life, said: 'I'm fine,' or 'Can't complain,' or 'Not bad,' when in reality they were angry, sad, frustrated or anxious, or any combination of emotions other than 'fine'. In fact, you may have heard this acronym:

F – freaked out
I – insecure
N – neurotic
E – emotional

So a little extra 'Are you sure?' can really go a long way in reassuring the person that you are there for them, and you aren't just asking out of politeness.

Create trust

Having a conversation forms a relationship between the speaker and the listener, and for this to be significant or impactful, trust must be involved. This can take time. Every conversation is different – and so is every person. Some people might take a while to open up or feel calm enough to speak. Some may be tearful and need a safe space to just cry it out. Some might want a hug, and others may not want any physical contact, but feel that you being there, nearby, is enough. For some, the initial overspill of emotion might lead to chaotic or confused feelings. Once emotions are unlocked, thoughts, words and ideas might come tumbling out and, initially, not seem to make much sense. But that's OK. What's important is just being there for someone so that they can let it all out – let the floodgates open. Then, once that valve is released, have confidence that the tap doesn't need to be switched back off until you feel it's right to do so.

Put yourself to one side

Remember that a good listener will put their own emotions, beliefs, experiences and reactions aside to allow the person speaking the space and confidence to continue, safe in the knowledge that they will not be judged. Sometimes, what you might hear may challenge you – it could go against your own long-held beliefs or just not quite make sense to you. But what's important here is helping the person who is telling you their problems to make sense of it themselves. The comfort of the speaker will grow if the listener's response – or anticipated response – is one of empathy as opposed to judgement.

Choose the right time and place

In the cut and thrust of daily life, there doesn't always seem to be the time or space to have an important talk. So, make sure you find the most appropriate place to have a conversation: somewhere that will help the other person feel comfortable and where you won't be interrupted. This will help them feel safe and let the conversation flow naturally. You might pop over to their place for a cup of tea and a chat, or go out for a walk or for a coffee. It might feel too confrontational and intense to say, 'Let's talk,' and then sit down face to face. Sometimes, the best conversations can be had while you're in the car, or doing the dishes, or out for a walk. Being side by side, and doing a simple task or something creative together can help build a sense of shared space that allows the other person to talk freely, without feeling any pressure (see 'Shoulder-to-shoulder therapy', page 73). Being active while you talk is also thought to open up deeper emotions which may be difficult to reach.

Being truly present for someone else can provide a healing balm in itself, giving them the validation that you understand that whatever it is they are going through is real and relevant. Offering them the time and space to be heard and recognised can show them that you acknowledge there is an issue, and this can give them the chance to let off steam, or admit to a problem, or speak in confidence. Then, through exploring and talking about what's going on, their feelings about it can begin to improve.

Little tips for helping someone open up

When someone is carrying around worries and difficult feelings, they can feel very lonely. You don't have to be an expert to help someone open up: the fact that you care is what matters.

If you're worried about someone, try using some of these conversation starters. If having an in-person conversation isn't possible, you can use the same principles when having a chat on the phone, video-calling someone or messaging them.

Here are some ideas to help start a tricky conversation:

• 'How are things? I've noticed you don't seem quite yourself.'
• 'Last week you mentioned that you were having a hard time dealing with…'
• 'I think I might have said something insensitive, so I just wanted to say sorry – I didn't realise things were so hard for you at the moment.'
• 'It seems like things might be hard right now. I just wanted you to know that I am here for you.'

Keeping the conversation going

Try to be open

If you've struggled in the past, or have supported someone else who has been through rough periods of mental health, it might help to mention that, but remember not to make the conversation about you.

Don't be afraid to ask questions

When we are worried about someone, we can spend a lot of time and energy trying to work out what they might need from us. But none of us are mind readers. Asking someone directly what could help them is a lot quicker and easier than playing a guessing game – and it will mean they get more of what they actually need. Even if they're not entirely sure how to answer, asking gives you an opportunity to work it out together.

Ask how the person feels. It sounds obvious, but sometimes people will talk you through all the facts of what happened, including why it happened and what actions they are thinking of taking, but never actually say how they feel about it.

Keep the conversation flowing and encourage them to keep talking until they can begin to work out the cause of their issues and figure out for themselves which is the next best step for them to take. You can do this by asking open questions (see page 81), summarising what they have said and reflecting on what you've heard them say. When you take a moment to check that you have understood what it is they're saying, this can clarify the point for the person who is speaking, too, and it can also help them to see if there's anything else that needs to be explored. Use small words of encouragement to help them keep going. Just saying 'Yep?' or, 'Is there anything else that you feel about that?' can be really helpful. As they start to describe and explain their thoughts and feelings, they will be more likely to understand the situation for themselves.

Don't be afraid of silence

Often, our thoughts are complex and difficult to articulate, so give the person you're listening to the space and time to gather their thoughts. Don't interrupt, and don't worry about pauses or gaps of silence in the conversation, as this can happen when they are thinking of the next thing they want to say. The idea is for them to keep talking until they have let it all out, and allowing a little silence can give them space to do that.

Reflect on what you've noticed

One part of the Samaritans listening model (page 186) is reflecting: picking up on something someone has said and saying it back to them. Sometimes they may make what appears to be a throwaway comment, and they may not even know they want to talk about that thing. But by saying, 'I noticed earlier, you said...', you give them a chance to reflect on it and then explore it a bit further if they want to. You can use the same principle to help someone open up initially, by reflecting that you've noticed they have been quieter than usual, seemed a bit down, haven't been coming into work as often as they usually would, or have stopped attending a joint activity. Reflecting your observation back to someone might prompt them to think more about what's going on for them, and it could encourage them to speak out.

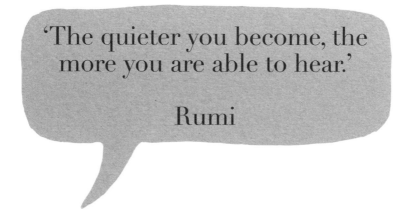

'The quieter you become, the more you are able to hear.'

Rumi

Don't be too hard on yourself

If you feel like you've said the wrong thing at any point during the conversation, don't panic – and don't be too hard on yourself if you feel like you've messed up. Just keep going and encourage the other person to keep talking, and you will be able to rectify the problem. If the conversation isn't working, give the other person space to absorb what's going on and time to respond. They might be unprepared to talk at that moment, but having the option to come back to you when they are ready will probably be a welcome one.

You can't force someone to accept help

Remember: you can only help someone when they're ready, so let them know you're there to listen when the time feels right for them. It's not easy to see someone you care for dealing with a difficult situation alone, and it's natural to want them to feel better. But they have to be at a stage where they want help. By forcing someone to talk before they are ready, you risk pushing them further away. If they know you are there, they will come to you when they feel ready and able.

Getting out and about can help people open up

I'm currently hiking around the country visiting every Samaritans branch in the United Kingdom and the Republic of Ireland for the Listening Walk. Whenever I meet someone, regardless of how they behave, I simply say 'How are you?' It's amazing how people feel unused to hearing those words.

The training is brilliant with Samaritans, because we learn to use soft questioning mixed in with a few hard questions. So you learn to challenge in the right way, to get people to think about what's going on with them. I've used those methods on the walk and I've had some amazing conversations with people just by inviting them to talk without any agenda. I'm not a trained therapist: I'm just a person who isn't scared of saying the wrong thing if someone tells me they're miserable. I just ask a question, and then they'll come back with an answer.

The conversations I'm having on the walk are not what I expected. I don't go straight into Samaritans mode: it's far more conversational. It's great to have open, meaningful conversations in more of a day-to-day setting. People are so rarely given the space and time to talk, and when they are it sort of jolts them into opening up. It's also quite rare that people are shown that sense that someone cares for them, particularly a stranger. Quite often, in the busy distractions of life, we forget to tell friends and family that we care, so to show up and offer to be there for a stranger seems to have real impact.

I've spoken face to face with all sorts of people, from ex-members of the armed forces who have suffered really badly with PTSD, to someone I met outside the toilet block of a campsite whose family member had been bereaved by suicide. I've bumped into famous actors and marathon runners who look as if they're the most successful people in the world, but have told me they're not feeling great, or have been going through difficult things in their lives. Sometimes I just say to them, 'There's nothing to say. I'm not going to give you any clichés. That must have been hard for you.' People might ask, 'Have you ever been through something similar?' and it's a very different situation to a Samaritans call, where we'd say 'It's not going to be helpful for you if I tell you all about my personal life.' In this situation, it's more conversational, so I might say, 'Yeah I did go through something a bit like that once. I'm OK now, but it was really difficult at the time.' You can sort of give more of yourself when it's in these more informal circumstances. The same would be true of a conversation with friends and family. I think me opening up is like giving them a little bit of the fishing line to help them catch the hook. I'd never make the conversation about me, but I think there's a value in someone realising you're a human too. They can see I have my own little anxieties, and that I'm approaching them from a place of honesty.

I don't mind a challenge. I've gone through all sorts of areas with my little backpack on and a flag stuck on an old fishing rod poking out the top. Once

I saw a bunch of lads outside a pub who weren't looking so sympathetic to the cause, but I couldn't just go past. I thought, I'm either going to get my head kicked in or they'll have a chance to speak. They were so surprised when I stopped to talk to them that we ended up having a really good conversation, and now they know where to get support if they ever need it. At the end, they said, 'Thanks for stopping, mate. Cheers. Good luck.'

I'm always so pleased that I just happened to be there at that time to talk to someone, and that I didn't panic at their response, because I know how much it's helped that person. I've handed out about 5,000 Samaritans cards since I've been walking. People have gone off clutching those little cards, as if they have given them a bit of hope.

Everybody's busy these days, but I've got the luxury of time on the walk, so I can stand with somebody for as long as I like – which is how it should be. We should all be thinking, Am I doing what's most important here? Sometimes, it's easy to lose sight of what it's all about.

Dave, a Samaritans volunteer from Doncaster

Shoulder-to-shoulder therapy

UKCP Psychotherapist Dr Christian Buckland

When it comes to helping someone talk, it is worth considering the different ways in which people communicate. Sometimes people will really open up in a letter, by email or on the phone, but find it harder to communicate face to face, so be mindful of this when listening. You could ask a friend if they would find it helpful to write down what they are feeling, for example.

When thinking about psychotherapy, it's common to imagine two people sitting face to face and talking. This is very often the case. However, eye contact can be experienced differently by different people. Some find it a positive experience, as it reassures them that they are being listened to, and it can help them to talk more freely, whereas others may find it intimidating and find it prevents them from opening up. Therapists often utilise different techniques to help with that, such as having chairs that swivel, which allow those patients who experience eye contact as anxiety-provoking to choose to turn and face away from the therapist. Other therapists may choose to allow the patient to lie down on a couch while they sit behind. Another option would be to have the chairs placed next to each other at an angle that does not promote direct eye contact. Techniques designed to alleviate difficult feelings related to eye contact can help promote a therapeutic technique called 'free association', which encourages the speaker to talk without interruption on any topic that comes to mind. This often helps to shine a spotlight on their unconscious processes, and can be helpful in understanding their inner psychological world.

Whereas a therapy session traditionally benefits from face-to-face interaction, when a friend opens up to you, they might find it easier to do so if they don't feel or see your judgement or reaction so keenly – for example, while walking and talking side by side. I have been told on numerous occasions that when people find they need to talk to their parents, friends, partners or children about a difficult topic, they will ask to go for a walk or for a drive. This can be a really good option, as the focus is not directly on the person talking, and there are other stimuli around. The listener is present and may find the topic easier to cope with. There is also an end to a walk or a drive, which helps the conversation come to a natural conclusion. Some people find this easier.

We can mirror the value of some of these listening techniques when listening to a friend or loved one: try having a conversation while sitting side by side, while you're doing the washing up or even, if safe to do so, while driving (or sitting) in a car. Sometimes this shoulder-to-shoulder listening can be really valuable in helping a person feel heard.

A psychotherapist's advice on having a hard conversation

• Let the other person take the lead.

• Avoid directing the conversation unnecessarily.

- Use facial expressions, verbal sounds and words to help the listener know you are listening and interested.

- Use their own words to repeat back to them what you have heard and to help them feel understood.

- Use encouraging phrases, such as 'Can you tell me a bit more about that?'

- Ask them to describe their experiences, and the physical sensations that they feel associated with the emotions they're dealing with.

- Be open to being corrected.

- Do not feel the need to understand every aspect of what they're saying: it is often more helpful to allow them to keep talking.

- If you are face to face, look for body language clues when they are speaking. Some studies suggest that only 7 per cent of communication is verbal, with the rest being 38 per cent vocal and 55 per cent visual.

- Offer empathy as well as sympathy. Try to put yourself in their position and imagine what they may be feeling.

You're not going to do any harm by asking someone how they're feeling

At Samaritans, we're not therapists. We're not trained counsellors. We're not angels or heroes. We're just real people, trained to listen to other people. And in doing so, we hope to help people find a way out of the darkness that they are experiencing in that moment. We don't aim to fix anyone and we're not saying that listening alone will save someone's life. What we are saying is that, for over 65 years, we have sat alongside those who need us, giving them the time and opportunity to be heard and helping them to process what they are going through. We hope that by doing this, they may eventually be ready to take steps to find their own way forwards.

The most important thing we provide is human contact: simply one person giving another person time, without distractions, to really try and understand how they are feeling in that moment. There's not always a crisis to discuss: it might be a daily worry or something specific that's troubling someone, or it could be a difficult feeling that they have been trying to manage alone for some time, but need a sounding board for. We listen without judgement. We do not problem-solve. We do not provide a solution. We allow people to share what may be a heavy load of thoughts so that they can start working through what some of their options might be, and remind themselves of their own feelings of self-worth.

If someone you know goes through something that's hard – such as loss, grief or a big life change – just send them a text to say, 'I've heard what's happened, how are you?' And although it might be more emotive or challenging, you have a head start if you know someone well. You're not going to do any harm by asking someone how they're feeling. Don't overthink it. If they just want you to sit with them, or give them a hug, then that's what you should do.

By allowing them to lead the conversation and share what is relevant to them, you can get a better idea of what they're going through. They know their situation best. By listening, you've started to help them move in the right direction. You might be able to ask them what support they are looking for, or help them identify possible coping strategies or consider next steps, such as getting a doctor's appointment.

Everybody experiences difficult feelings at some point, and we all need to learn positive rather than negative ways of coping with these feelings and emotions. There seems to be this idea that we always need to be happy and well-rounded, with good mental health. But life isn't like that, is it? All of us dip up and down. Dealing with anxiety and feeling anxious is part of life. It isn't possible to prevent someone you care about from ever being anxious, and it's not actually helpful to try and do that. What you can do is help them learn that they can cope with feeling this way. It's about letting them say, 'I'm having a bit of a rubbish day today and I'm not feeling very good.' Then you can prompt them into thinking, 'So, what will I do about it? How am I going to look after myself?' It's about helping someone develop strategies to help them manage whatever life throws at them.

What we know as Samaritans volunteers is how important it is to enable somebody to make their own decisions, and to let them know that we will still be there for them whatever they decide. Showing you are listening is actually about holding up a mirror and reflecting back what that person is really saying. Good listening isn't just about nodding along: it's about engaging, and maybe being brave enough to reflect back what you've heard. It's about listening intently enough to genuinely pick up on something and then giving an empathetic response that shows you've taken it in.

When you ask someone if they want to talk, they might just need to vent and offload and then they're done. Or the conversation you have may be the catalyst for them realising they need to seek further help and make significant changes in their life.

Jayne, Samaritans volunteer for 25 years

'Helping a person will not necessarily change the world, but it can change the world for that person.'

Anonymous

Chapter 6:
Learning to listen

'SHUSH' listening tips

As Samaritans volunteers, we seek to listen and to understand. This enables us to begin the journey of helping the person we are talking to understand that rock bottom doesn't always mean full stop. That there is always another choice. But you don't have to be an expert to help someone who's having a tough time. Simply listening can help someone work through how they're feeling. Take a moment to learn how to be a better listener with our 'SHUSH' listening tips.

S – Show you care.
H – Have patience.
U – Use open questions.
S – Say it back.
H – Have courage.

S – Show you care

Give the person you are listening to your full, undivided attention. This is a non-verbal way of showing them how much you care. To really listen to somebody, you need to give them your full attention and be engaged. So focus on the other person: make eye contact, put away your phone and use positive, open body language. Life can be extremely busy and, in this age of constant digital connectivity, multitasking has become the norm. We love our phones, but it's important to set yours to one side while you're listening, turning it off or putting it on silent to stop you getting distracted. Try to really focus on learning something new about the person who is talking.

Maintaining eye contact with the person you're listening to can show you're interested in what they're saying and that they have your full attention (although excessive eye contact can come across to some people as threatening, so be mindful of staring). But if the person doesn't feel comfortable meeting your gaze or holding eye contact, then that's OK – don't feel under pressure to look them in the eye. Watch their mouth or hands instead, or look in the same direction they're facing. This works best if you sit alongside the person you're speaking with, rather than head on (see page 73). But remember, they might occasionally look to see if you are still listening, so keep focus.

We all use body language at an unconscious level. It's part of how we communicate with others: we are constantly dropping clues about what's going on in our heads, often without realising what signals we are giving. When two people are in tune with one another, they will often mirror each other's body language. Here are some ways you can express positive body language:

- Try sitting at a five o'clock angle to the person you're supporting.
- Lean forward slightly to show you are interested in what the other person is saying.
- Be aware of any habits you have which might be off-putting, like glancing at your watch or phone.
- Be careful not to fidget.
- Keep your arms open and uncrossed.
- Sit or stand at the same level, so you're not looking up or down at the person you're listening to, as this might make you both feel uncomfortable.
- Try not to let your mood or how you're feeling show in your body language. Be aware of what your body is doing and the signals you're giving.

H – have patience

It may take time and several attempts before a person is ready to open up. This may not be achieved in your first conversation, but each interaction can be helpful in building up a sense of safety and trust.

Effective listening is about showing compassion and creating trust, and patience is key.

The person sharing shouldn't feel rushed. If they do, they won't feel it's a safe environment. If they've paused in their response, wait: they may not have finished speaking. It might take them some time to formulate what they want to say, or they may find it difficult to articulate what they're feeling. Through non-judgemental listening, you are allowing the person to relax into the conversation and use it as a place to reflect or work through difficult emotions.

Don't interrupt or cut in. Let the conversation wind and travel – meandering down thought pathways is often how someone might end up at a revelation that surprises even themselves and allows them to form a new conclusion or opinion about their situation. If someone pauses, count to five in your head. Letting the pause happen will help give the other person clarity, space to think and time to elaborate further if they need to. It also shows you are thinking about what they are saying, which will hopefully give them the confidence they need to keep talking.

U – Use open questions

Opening up about a problem can be difficult. Someone might start by telling you about a smaller, separate issue they may have been having, or they might talk about what they're going through, but initially downplay how they're really feeling. They might not even know what the heart of the problem is until they have explored it with you.

Often people want to talk, but will wait until someone asks how they are. Questions that invite someone to elaborate rather than just giving a 'yes' or 'no' answer are the most useful. Instead of closing the conversation down, open questions encourage the other person to keep talking and explore how they're feeling. An open question demonstrates that you want to listen and that you care.

Try asking, 'How are you feeling today?' and then following it up with 'Tell me more about that.' Inviting the person to elaborate or asking questions which cannot be answered monosyllabically will give them the chance to tell you more. These questions don't impose a viewpoint or imply any judgement. They require the other person to pause, think and reflect, and then hopefully expand.

Here are some examples of open questions:

• When – 'When did you realise you felt this way?'
• Where – 'Where did that happen?' or 'Where do you go when you start to feel anxious?'
• What – 'What else happened?' or 'What do you think is making you feel this way?'
• How – 'How did that feel?'

Be careful with 'why' questions, as they can sometimes suggest judgement and make the other person feel defensive. Instead of saying 'Why did you do that?', try saying 'What made you choose that?' or 'What were you thinking about at the time?' These questions are more open and effective and will help the person you're listening to feel able to explore safely.

Using open questions encourages the other person to talk, and shows them that the conversation is a safe space where nothing they say is right or wrong. With active listening, although you do some talking, you're really acting as a sounding board. Whatever you say shouldn't influence what the other person has to say. It should just help them to talk.

S – Say it back

Check you've understood, but don't interrupt or offer a solution. Repeating something back to somebody is a really good way to reassure them that they have your undivided attention. And you can check to see that you're hearing what they want you to hear, not putting your own interpretation on to the conversation.

Saying it back is an opportunity to ask someone if you have understood them properly. It shows that you are listening intently and trying to understand what they are feeling from their point of view rather than your own. Mirroring the language they are using also demonstrates that you care about what they are saying or trying to say in their words. It also gives them a chance to reflect on what they've said, which can lead to further exploration of a thought or idea that they can then elaborate on.

H – Have courage

Don't be put off by a negative response and don't be afraid of silence. As we have already discussed, you don't have to fill gaps in the conversation.

Sometimes it can feel intrusive or counter-intuitive to ask someone how they feel. You'll soon be able to tell if someone is uncomfortable and doesn't want to engage with you at that level, and that can help you feel more confident with asking in the first place. You'll be surprised by how often people are willing or even eager to talk, and how, sometimes, being asked how they feel is exactly what somebody needs in order to be able to share what is going on in their mind.

Elaboration task

For this task, give yourself a rule to gently ask the other person to elaborate until there's nothing more to say. For example, if someone says, 'I feel low,' the conversation might go like this:

Listener: 'Tell me more about feeling low.'
Speaker: 'Well, everything feels black.'
Listener: 'Tell me about the black.'
Speaker: 'Well, thick, dense, velvety black.'
Listener: 'Can you tell me when that happens to you?'
Speaker: 'It happens in the morning.'
Listener: 'Tell me about black mornings.'

So you're constantly saying, 'Tell me more', 'I want to understand it more.' Keep going until you absolutely can't find another question to ask.

What stops us from listening well?

UKCP Psychotherapist Dr Christian Buckland

One of the main barriers to people listening well is a lack of confidence. People often think 'Yeah, but what can I do?' and then shy away from attempting to help. You might worry about what you are going to do if you ask someone if they're OK, and they say they're not. You might wonder if you are equipped with the right tools to help them, or you might be worried you'll make it worse. But it's important to know that, when offering to listen to somebody, you don't have to know any answers. You do not need to fix things or to give a solution, or find any kind of answer. Actually, it's much simpler than that. If you can just be there to listen and provide a space for someone else to talk; if you can ask someone to elaborate and encourage them to keep the flow of conversation going, eventually they will work out the solution to their problem by themselves. Listening to somebody's problems doesn't make you responsible for solving them.

Barriers to listening

Listening is so underrated. It is not about simply possessing good communication skills. It involves taking a genuine interest in the other person, showing a desire to get to know them and a willingness to put them first. Many people face challenges to listening well, which can include:

Our need to help
It can feel natural to want to rescue someone who is talking and appears to be distressed. This can often lead the listener to interject and direct the conversation.

The need to be in control
Often listeners find themselves either consciously or unconsciously preoccupied with feelings such as anxiety or fear, which can lead them to direct the conversation in a manner that reduces their own anxiety.

Conditional regard
The listener may find the subject matter difficult to hear and may need to change the subject. See page 179 for more on this.

Unconscious bias
The listener may not be aware of their own bias relating to specific groups outside of their own conscious awareness. Without realising it, the listener might make judgements about what they're hearing.

Making assumptions
We live in a fast-paced world where we like to skim-read headlines and often miss important facts. It can be too easy to make a quick assumption regarding the speaker's narrative or their feelings.

Forgetting that every person's story is unique
It can be easy to forget that everyone's life experiences are different. Just because a story is similar to one we have heard before does not mean that the person's experience will be the same, or even similar.

Being distracted by our own lived experiences
In a desire to be helpful, it can be extremely tempting to find parallels between the story the person is sharing and our own personal experiences. This can result in us wanting to share our own story, which is often extremely unhelpful for the other person and can lead to feelings of unimportance and being dismissed.

Use compassion

One of the most important components in listening well is compassion. Compassionate connection is based on respect and dignity; it draws on empathy, kindness and patience – towards yourself as well as those around you. It can improve your health, boost your wellbeing, and strengthen your relationships. While empathy is the ability to put yourself in the other person's place and understand their distress, compassion has the additional element of actively wanting to support them. This doesn't mean you have to try and solve their problems for them – it's about actively being there for them as they work towards a solution.

The compassion shown to someone can affect how they perceive their interactions with others and can make them feel valued and cared for. Most significantly, showing compassion is a skill that can be learned. Acting compassionately just relies on you being able to relate to someone else's emotional state and, crucially, wanting to support them.

How to show compassion

- Be kind and show you care however you can – from offering someone a cup of tea to going and visiting them.

- Ask the person how they are and demonstrate that you are listening to them with focus and care.

- Use words of encouragement, as well as open body language and reassuring physical gestures.

- If someone is comfortable with it, give them a hug or hold their hand. Others may be less comfortable with physical contact, and that's OK too – always be respectful of someone's boundaries.

- Encourage people to keep talking by nodding and showing you are interested.

- Repeat back to someone what you are hearing to show you are listening.

- Be an advocate for mental health issues and avoid using patronising or disrespectful terms.

Talking about a problem can alleviate the burden

Victoria lives in London. She began to experience anxiety when she had to travel a lot for her job and found herself alone, in new cities, with no routine. 'When you're on your own so much of the time, it can be really isolating,' she says. 'Sometimes I'd be away for weeks at a time, and I was just so lonely. I felt like I never had any control about where the next flight was going, or how to get to an airport or hotel by myself in a new place, or where to go out and get food. It became as if I didn't have any control over how I was feeling, either.'

Victoria had caring friends and a supportive family, but as her anxiety escalated, she became convinced that they wouldn't be able to hear what she had to say. 'One of the reasons I called Samaritans was because I didn't want to burden my friends with the things I was going through. I didn't want to take up their time, alter the way they were with me or lean on them too much because I thought they had enough going on themselves.' Another thing that stopped Victoria reaching out to her friends was a fear of judgement. 'I like to think I'm fun and outgoing and a laugh, and I'm happy being like that with my friends.'

But with hindsight, she wishes she had reached out to the people that were there for her before things got so bad.

Victoria's thoughts became so troubling that she was frightened by what she was thinking and feeling. In that distorted reality, everything felt terrifying. She began having panic attacks, sometimes having to get off the bus on her way to work because she felt as if she couldn't breathe. Even though Victoria was aware of the stress she was under, she felt like she couldn't prevent it. 'When you have a panic attack, you're really fixated on how to stop it from happening, which makes you more stressed. It then becomes harder and harder to pull yourself out of it and calm down.'

While Victoria didn't feel like she was suicidal at the time, she ended up in a situation where she realised she was contemplating ending her life. 'It's kind of a blur in my head, but I just remember feeling terrified on my way home from work one day. I was thinking, Surely this is not what my life is. I just didn't want to hear my own thoughts anymore. I didn't want to deal with any of the stuff I was feeling. I thought, There is an easy way for it to just be gone. I didn't go out that day thinking that's what I was going to do, or that's where I would end up. It wasn't an active decision. But for some reason, after standing somewhere where, with one step I could have ended it all, and thinking about taking my own life for quite a while, I just went home. I honestly can't even tell you why I didn't go through with it. It scared me because I'd never experienced that kind of feeling before.'

Victoria's housemates were aware she was distressed, but didn't know what to do. 'That night was awful. I was just sobbing and sobbing. I didn't call any of my friends, I went on Google and typed in "Who can I speak to if I need help?" and, thank goodness, the number for Samaritans came up. Without that, I honestly don't know what would have happened.'

When Victoria phoned Samaritans that evening, she says she felt relief, as if a huge weight had been lifted off her shoulders. 'I just let it all out. I spoke about things that I didn't even realise were bothering me. I was freaking out, but the guy on the other end of the phone was so calm and patient. It made me calmer. I didn't feel like he was judging me in any way. I can't remember what I said to him. I was crying a lot; I don't even know how he understood what I was saying. But the longer I was on the phone, the more he was allowing me to get my feelings out and talk, which I did eventually. He got me to the point where I could say, "OK, I'm OK now. I can breathe." At the end of the call, he said, "Whenever you're ready, you can put the phone down. We won't put the phone down on you." It was nice to know that it was my decision. I remember saying, "Thank you so much. I can sleep now." And I did.'

Victoria recalls that being listened to held her in a safe place where she felt able to say whatever she wanted without anyone judging her or telling her what to do. This gave her back the power to realise that actually, maybe she could find her own way out of the problems she was having, and that allowed her to begin to move in a direction where she was able to cope.

'By being willing to listen to me and hear what I had to say, that Samaritans volunteer made me feel validated. He made me feel like I was worthy of carrying on. He gave me a bit of purpose. I thought, He gave me the time to talk and if he can give me that, then I can give myself a chance to wake up tomorrow and see what happens. And actually, when I woke up the next day, I felt so much better. I think it was literally just getting it all out, which made a huge amount of difference. It took a long while after that, to get to a point where I was OK. But that was the first step forward. And – touch wood – I've not been back to that point since.'

Victoria's guidance on helping someone talk through their problems

• Have the confidence to begin a tricky conversation. What's the worst that could happen?

• One thing that worked really well for me was that a friend and I would visit art galleries. We both love art, and every single time we went, we'd end up talking about our feelings. That was like our safe space. I found the same thing in my running group, too. Being alongside someone allows you to open up much more and you end up talking about more meaningful things, just by sharing physical space.

• Don't worry about saying something wrong.

• You don't need to fix anything – just be there.

• Read up. Educate yourself around things like panic attacks and anxiety.

• Routinely check in. Even if you think someone is absolutely fine, just say. 'I want you to know that I'm here for you. You don't have to talk to me, and I can't make you talk about your feelings. But I want you to know that I'm here whenever you need me.'

Good listening is something you can learn

Good listening isn't necessarily something that comes naturally to us, but it's something that can be learned and improved upon. It's among the first skills that we develop as human beings… and then we learn to talk. And that's it: suddenly, it's all about 'me'. Let me interrupt. I want to tell you what I know. I'm listening to what you're saying, but actually, I'm just waiting for you to finish talking so that I can tell you what I think.

When you're with friends and family, you often cue up a response ready for when they finish talking, because you have an opinion about what they are saying. You want to say your piece. But what's actually happened is that you have stopped listening and you're on autopilot, just waiting for your chance to reply.

The more you learn to apply good listening practices, the more your brain starts to adapt. At first, you have to try hard to remember that it doesn't really matter what you've got to say. This takes effort and persistence. Remind yourself to concentrate on what the other person is saying. That's what's really important: to let them finish their sentences and give them the space to say what they need to.

Hearing is not the same as listening. I can hear a song on the radio. I can hear someone cutting the grass outside, and children playing – but I'm not really taking it in. Whereas listening is being switched on to what the person who is speaking is telling you; it's remembering things, perhaps storing them in your mind because you want to come back to them later; it's trying to get a sense of the other person's situation and perspective.

I'm not saying this is easy. I think one of the trickiest things for friends and family to do is to remain impartial about what you're saying. It's not our natural standpoint, because we want to help. You have to constantly remind yourself to take a step backwards, to not jump in with ideas or fixes, and instead to simply listen. This essentially means not taking sides or forming strong opinions – which is hard to do when you are a worried relative, or a concerned friend.

Be mindful about giving an opinion unless it's asked for, as you could unintentionally set up a barrier between you and the person you're talking to. For example, if someone is telling you about an issue with their partner, you saying something like 'I think you could do so much better' might actually make the person feel as if you're judging them, and it's unlikely to help. It's almost a mindful practice, setting your own thoughts and opinions aside and simply asking what they want to do. Being able to talk through their options in this way will empower them to make the best decision for themselves.

An important part of being a good listener is focusing your attention. We all have the ability to clear our minds and concentrate on the present moment. One of the most important things is to try and make sure you're not distracted by anything else that's going on around you, such as other family members or people coming in and out. Try to give all your attention to the person you're listening to. Having uninterrupted time to talk is key. If you do lose track of the conversation at any point, simply ask the person you're talking with to repeat what they've just said, and apologise if you didn't quite catch something. It's always best to check points, and it might help clarify what the person is thinking about. You can always ask open questions that allow you to delve further, or probe deeper into the issues that most need exploring.

As well as noticing if someone is feeling low, or lethargic, you might notice the opposite: that someone is over-active, or that their energy is a lot more lively than usual. In these cases, it can help to use your energy to balance someone else's, speaking calmly, quietly and slowly.

This is a technique used by counsellors and therapists, but the principles can be used just as easily with friends and family. Use small gestures and words of encouragement – it can be as simple as saying 'Yeah… that's rubbish,' or nodding your head in empathy. Make sure your body language is open and approachable. It all helps to demonstrate that you are listening intently, and open to understanding what someone is telling you.

Lucia, Samaritans listening volunteer

Chapter 7:
Don't give advice

There's no need to give a solution

In everyday life, it's easy to offer little bits of guidance and advice here and there without much thought. But with important or difficult decisions, telling someone what to do can be unhelpful. The best support you can provide is helping them talk through the problems they are facing so that they can decide what's best for them. Allow people to make their own decisions wherever possible – telling people what to do takes responsibility away from them.

There is a common misconception that listening to someone means that you need to help fix what they are going through by coming up with a solution. Perhaps you might think it will be quicker to give someone advice about what you might do or have done in similar situations in the past. But by telling someone what you think they should do, you are invalidating what they are going through. By talking about yourself, you aren't listening to and accepting what the person is saying, and you aren't responding to what they are trying to tell you. The minute you switch into 'fix' mode, you are talking about yourself and your opinions and ideas, which can cause others to retreat, thinking, Why am I bothering? The risk then is that they will close up and be unwilling to talk further.

When people are going through times of difficulty, they often experience feelings of powerlessness. Low confidence and low self-esteem can cause a cycle of negative thinking. They might think they are a burden, bad at everything and completely useless. If you jump straight in and try to fix their problem for them, they might feel as if you're saying, 'Yeah, actually, you're not good enough to fix this yourself, because I'm having to do it for you.' This can feed into those feelings of powerlessness and self-doubt, with the person perceiving that you don't think they're capable of dealing with things themselves. For someone trapped in a negative thought cycle whose self-worth is already low, this can be really damaging.

Reassure them that they are not a burden, and understand that all that person wants from you is for you to sit with them and be there for them in that moment. That might feel like a tricky thing to ask for in the melting pot of emotion and context and history that you have with the people who know you best. But from the point of view of the person that's struggling, they need to remain in control to realise that they have the answers within themselves. Help them think of all the options available to them, but leave the choice about what to do up to them. Invariably, people do know what they need to do, they just haven't been able to think it through, or haven't had the chance to articulate it.

If you're struggling with the urge to give advice or offer solutions, try asking questions like these instead:

- How does this make you feel?
- Can you remember when this problem first began? How did it become an issue?
- What would be the best realistic outcome for you, do you think?
- Can you think of anything that might make you feel better?
- Do you have any ways of feeling less worried about the situation?
- Do you think there's anything you could do to change the situation?
- How effective do you think that would be?
- Would something like that be feasible for you?

Have open, honest conversations

Steven, 36, is from Kilmarnock. When his mum and dad split up in his youth, he moved countries and schools and became the man of the house at a young age. Then, at 16, he became ill with a virus that left him in a wheelchair. Later, one of Steven's friends took his own life, and Steven began having problems at work that left him feeling stressed. But having never spoken about his emotions before, Steven wasn't able to understand that his brain was trying to process a lot of distressing information, without any coping strategies.

'Everybody will face struggles at some point, whether it's losing a loved one, or losing a job, dealing with a financial problem, or whatever – but nobody ever tells you what it can feel like when you're struggling,' he says. 'So until something bad happens, you don't have any frame of reference. There's no preparation, and so suddenly you're hit with it, and you don't know what to do.'

Steven didn't want to burden his friends and family by putting his feelings on to them. 'I don't know whether it's society or whether it's just something that's in guys' heads, but there's still this idea that, as a man, you want to be a provider and a protector. Obviously, we've moved on from whacking a bear over the head with a club and dragging it home for dinner, but for some reason we still feel we must protect. I didn't want to say anything to my partner or those around me about how I was feeling, because I thought it would hurt her or cause them distress – and I didn't want anyone to worry about me. If I hadn't been thinking that way, maybe my problems wouldn't have got so bad so fast.'

In retrospect, Steven wishes that he had admitted he was finding things tough earlier. 'If I had spoken to somebody before I started self-harming, for example, it would have been a lot easier. But I hadn't even told anyone I was struggling to cope. I thought if I told them what I was doing, I would face shock and disgust. People's faces give away what they're thinking and those micro-expressions can be so big to somebody that's on high alert.'

At the time, Steven didn't know how to talk about his feelings, and was worried about how people might react, or what they might say. 'Sometimes it felt like I was saying, "I've been to Tenerife," and the other person would say, "Oh, but I've been to Eleven-erife." It was like a sort of one-upmanship. Saying "I feel bad" might be met with a response like, "Yeah, but my experience was way worse than that," which really wasn't helpful. It would stop me from opening up more. Even if the sentiment comes from a good place, even if they're just trying to find common ground and show that they have experienced something similar, it isn't useful if you're trying to talk and someone else takes over.'

When he was struggling with mental health issues, Steven felt as if everything was already outside of his control, so someone trying to take control and care for him made the situation worse. 'It felt like it was just confirming that I couldn't do it myself. I was telling myself all the time I couldn't do things because I was worthless, because I couldn't cope. So then someone saying, "I'm going to do it for you" really reaffirmed what I thought and left me feeling powerless.'

When Steven's thoughts were completely out of control, anything anybody said was turned into a negative. So even when people said they loved him, he thought, No you don't, how can you love somebody like this? or, You're only saying that because you don't want to feel guilty. Even the most caring actions were unintentionally exacerbating the negative things that Steven was telling himself. Unfortunately, his feelings worsened until he felt like he couldn't go on. He had an argument with his partner and was at home alone, with his thoughts running wild, and he made an attempt to take his own life. 'I think I knew I didn't actually want to die; I just wanted the distress and the turmoil and everything that I was feeling to stop. I didn't know any other way of coping with how I was feeling.' And so he picked up the phone, and called Samaritans. He was then taken to hospital in an ambulance.

'I remember when I phoned, I didn't say anything for a while. The person on the phone was just saying things like, "My name is... what's caused to you phone today?" And then he just waited for a wee while, until I could talk. I just felt so reassured that somebody was there. He was completely in the moment and that allowed me to finally formulate my own ideas, thoughts and issues. There was no judgement, or shock, or disgust. There was no "Right, this is what you need to do," or "This is what works for me," or "You just need to just snap out of it." In the first five minutes of the call, the Samaritans volunteer probably only said about ten words. Which meant it was all about me, and what I was feeling. It wasn't about the listener; it was about the speaker. And that was invaluable. It made me realise that, actually, I had the answers to my own questions and I did have control over what I was thinking and doing.'

Steven went on to spend seven months in a psychiatric hospital. But what he found was that, alongside all the clinical care and treatment he was receiving, something far simpler became the turning point for him in his recovery. 'I was surrounded by psychiatric nurses, psychologists and social workers. But the person who made the biggest difference to me was an auxiliary nurse. Every morning, she would come in and say "Hiya, good morning!" and I would either ignore her, or just grunt, or say "What's so good about it?" But every single morning, she would come back and say "Good morning!" The fact that she returned and persevered, being cheerful and encouraging me just to say "Hi" back to her every single day, eventually made me feel like she believed that I was a good person and that I was just ill. It wasn't the psychiatrists, it wasn't the psychologists, it wasn't the psychiatric nurses that have years of training, specifically in mental health. It was the auxiliary nurse that opened the blinds and made me realise that I was worth saying good morning to.'

Steven's guidance for open, honest conversations

• For me, one of the most powerful things about the Samaritans listening service that you can take into day-to-day life is the sense of someone just being in the moment with you. I knew somebody was there and willing to listen, and that they cared about what was happening to me.

• If someone you love is struggling, it's natural to want to help, but the best advice I can give you is to relinquish control. Allow someone to make their mistakes. And if that means them hitting rock bottom, the most important thing you can do is be there to help them pick up the pieces. That will do far less damage than saying: 'I know what's best for you because I know you best, and so I'm going to tell you what to do.' Because actually, by saying that, you're pushing the person away. You're saying: 'I don't trust you to do this yourself.'

• If you suspect someone is using self-harm as a coping strategy, look up some information on it first as this could help you understand more, and help you manage your reaction. Take time to prepare yourself before you have a conversation.

Research and read about mental health conditions – there is a lot of information out there on everything from low moods to diagnosable disorders.

- Don't be scared to say the words 'suicide' or 'self-harm' – they're not dirty words. If you speak them out loud, it's a way of showing that there's no judgement on your part, and that you're willing to have an open conversation. Just because you say something out loud, it won't lead to it happening. Often it can be a real relief for people to realise that they can express how they are feeling honestly and openly, and that can be really helpful.

- Don't forget that if you ask the question, you have to be prepared for the response. So don't ask how someone is if you're too busy or have too much going on to be able to listen properly. Make sure you have time to offer, even if that's saying, 'I can't chat properly now, but can I call you later? Or we can go for a coffee tomorrow?'

- Trust your gut. If you feel like someone you know is acting differently, just check in and send a message to see if they're OK. I mean, if I did it to my mates, there would probably be a fair few expletives in there too, but at least I'd be reaching out.

- I think encouraging guys to open up and share a bit is about perseverance. Just say something like: 'I noticed you've not been your usual chirpy self recently,' and leave it open. I would be very, very surprised if someone's immediate response was 'Oh, well let me tell you everything,' but it's about showing someone you are there to listen if and when they do want to talk, and that you do care. In my experience, that persistence shows that you genuinely want to hear what they've got to say.

It's enough to just be there for somebody

It would be great if everybody could go through a Samaritans training programme and apply it to their everyday life. I've been through the process twice. It was just utterly invaluable: I learned a huge amount and have taken it from that training back into my day-to-day life.

Letting people know they have support can be enough. There are places where you can go for more expert input, and sometimes people need to be carefully guided towards the GP for counselling, medication or CBT. But a big part of listening is about building up trust and creating a connection within a safe space. As a Samaritans volunteer, you don't just jump straight into the tricky stuff. You spend time building a rapport, establishing trust and getting the person to feel comfortable.

In everyday life, it's a lot harder. There are so many other things pressing in on you. But it's just about finding the right space, stopping what you're doing and trying to clear your mind and focus on what they are saying to you. It might take a little bit of time and practice to get there, but there is definitely a way to translate Samaritans training into normal life situations. I think anybody can become a better listener. Some people are more naturally inclined to it, but we can all improve our listening skills. It's just not something we're taught. I went to an all-boys school and there you really didn't talk about your feelings – so listening skills were never something I'd really understood before doing Samaritans training.

It's enough just to be there for somebody. That can be infinitely more valuable than trying to give advice. Just being there keeps the other person grounded and held in that moment – and that's often the starting point for turning things around.

There are some really practical things you can do, like speaking in a slower, calmer and more collected way. If you know someone well, you will naturally respond with more emotion than when speaking to a stranger, but you can try and balance that in your approach. The principle of being non-judgemental is important, too. You can't bring your own attitudes and opinions into listening. If someone feels vulnerable or overwhelmed by opening up, as a listener you want to avoid putting too much of yourself into the situation. Adding your own experiences and opinions is just introducing noise.

There is a perception that men in particular find it hard to open up. When I think back to my experience in school, I just wasn't given the vocabulary to do it, so it's an uncomfortable feeling. You're conditioned to feel you have to be strong and capable. There does seem to be much greater awareness now of the importance of talking about emotional and mental health, but unless that's demonstrated for you by a role model, it's difficult to know where to start. There is a way of challenging it, and saying that we can and should talk to one another more honestly, and that if we did, the negative feelings wouldn't get as bad as they sometimes do. But you have to trust that when you say those things, you're not going to be ridiculed for them. You need to know you're going to find the right support.

Finding the right setting is helpful, too. It's unlikely you'll have a good conversation about something important in a big group; there is a need for privacy to create a sense of confidentiality. Ask, 'Are you OK?' and then ask, 'But are you really?' The simplest things are often the best. Just letting someone know you are trying to reach out to them can be validating in itself. It's about opening up an avenue to say, 'If you want to talk, I'm here; if you want to talk to someone else, maybe do that.' Keep it natural, and keep it warm.

Listening is so important because people want to be heard. I know how good it makes me feel when I'm heard, and I know how that positive experience keeps me moving forward. If we all have that kind of experience then, actually, we could be in a much healthier and more sustainable place as a society.

Phil Selway, Radiohead drummer, was a Samaritans volunteer

You don't need to fix anything when listening

Michael, 31, is from Sheffield. At 18, he left school to join the military, but unfortunately was made redundant four years later. 'I had no idea what else I wanted to do,' he says. 'I felt like the one thing I knew was being taken away from me. All I had ever wanted for 10 years of my life was to fly aircraft in the military and now, through no fault of my own, I felt like I was failing. I just didn't have the resources to cope.

'As an officer, I was told, this is how you lead, this is how you solve problems, this is how we come up with solutions. It was all about problem-solving. So when I left the military and became unwell, trying to explore why I was ill, how I dealt with that and how my parents could try and support me was hard because there were so many unknowns.'

Part of Michael's redundancy package meant that he left day-to-day military service and started an undergraduate degree. For the first year, he experienced university the same way most people did: he had a laugh and went out four or five nights a week, drinking and socialising. Because he didn't officially leave the military until the end of his first university year, he still had a full salary, and was in regular contact with senior officers, who were monitoring his progress as part of the redundancy package. But after the ceremonial dinner to mark him leaving the armed forces, he returned to his life in Sheffield and it suddenly hit him that his support network wasn't there anymore. 'At the back of my mind, I was still an officer in the military and I still had that network of friends and colleagues that gave me a huge sense of belonging. But then all of a sudden, I was a 23-year-old at university with no income. I didn't know what I was doing with my life. As a result, my first real romantic relationship broke down, and so I lost that support, too.'

Michael tried to reinvent himself, taking on various roles and activities to distract himself, including internships, volunteering, running, sports clubs and a part-time job – all while trying to study. But in November of that year, he says he just broke. 'I went from knowing I was down, fed up and stressed, to not being able to leave the house. I didn't eat, I couldn't leave my room, I drank far too much, I wasn't looking after myself at all. Until that point, I thought I had to just keep pushing through, because that was how I'd always lived. The military had told me I might undergo periods of stress, but that as an officer, you have to make decisions and keep going, and that's how my mindset had been moulded from the ages of 13 to 22. But that feeling of breaking was really bad. I knew something was wrong.'

Although Michael was aware that things weren't right, he articulated it as feeling stressed and 'having a lot on'. But one night, he felt like he couldn't take it anymore. 'I was on a night out, under the influence of alcohol, and in an environment that I'd been in every Wednesday for the previous year. But I suddenly felt enormously overwhelmed and anxious. I just had to leave. There were loads of people around, but I didn't want to talk to or see anyone, so I ran down this alleyway and hid. That was the first time I called Samaritans. I can't remember exactly what I spoke about. All I remember is a massive sense of the anxiety easing. I went from being crouched over, cowering, bawling my eyes out down a dark alley to, 45 minutes or an hour later, being able to pick myself up, leave that place and go home. I had a proper night's sleep for the first time in ages. And the following day, I got up, went to the university student support service desk and said, "Can I speak to someone please? I'm not very well."

'Making that phone call to Samaritans was like lessening the acute crisis or stress that I was feeling at that time. I remember a sense of relief, but it was because I was letting it all out, not because I'd found a solution or someone was telling me what I should do. No one said "It's OK, it's over now, you're going to be alright." The question I was asked was: "Do you think you're going to be OK to carry on for the rest of the day or the rest of the evening?" There was no pretence that I would wake up tomorrow and everything would be fine, but it helped me see that I could function enough to get through the day and, eventually, that led me to believe that I could continue to exist.'

The instinct of Michael's parents was to come and pick him up, try and make him feel safe, provide the tea and biscuits, and help with practical support. But because of his depression and state of mind, when they told him that he was loved, all he could hear was someone not agreeing with him. 'I'm not saying they shouldn't have said it, because it was valuable. But I felt like they couldn't hear what I was saying to them. What I heard was that what I was feeling wasn't OK and wasn't normal, and I needed to do something to make those behaviours and those feelings acceptable. So many of us, when we try to listen, will immediately respond with what we think might be a solution. I just needed them to hear and acknowledge what I was feeling, not necessarily try and communicate anything back.

'If someone is feeling anxious or stressed, or if they've got low mood or low self-worth, by shutting down the exploration in a conversation and trying to solve it instead – even with the best of intentions – you're inadvertently compounding what they're already feeling: that they aren't good enough to sort themselves out. And that can make things worse.'

Good listening isn't just about hearing someone's words: it's also about how you respond to them. Michael felt that, although his parents listened, they didn't necessarily take in what he was saying, because their responses didn't mirror what he was feeling. 'It must be so hard for your parents, or your partner, to hear someone they love and care about so deeply articulate themselves with such little self-worth, and no positive outlook. It's totally understandable that they wanted to fix me and bring me back to being the person that had self-confidence and could understand what I was bringing to others. But actually, even if they did nothing at all other than just being there, allowing me to talk would have helped. It felt like they just didn't understand how I was feeling. I felt like they didn't get me, or what I was going through – like I was saying one thing and they were saying the opposite, which just reinforced the feeling that I was worthless, because I couldn't fix it myself.'

After a few months, with the help of medication, Michael returned to Sheffield, where he was able to access counselling through the university. 'I had my sessions with a university counsellor, and it changed my outlook. I managed to finish my second and third year.'

Michael has since had ups and downs with his mental health, but is more aware of the importance of spotting the signs earlier, which means he is able to reach out for help and talking therapies before the point of crisis. 'For me, the clinical kind of help always feels like a short- to medium-term fix; something to sufficiently reintegrate you back into normal life. But I remember when I first called Samaritans, it didn't feel like that. There was never any direction of conversation from the person on the end of the phone, and I never felt like they were trying to fix me. They were simply allowing me the opportunity to fully express how I was feeling in that given moment, and then subtly exploring how I felt. It allowed me to self-explore, and bring myself back from crisis, as opposed to someone saying "We're going to try and fix you immediately." I'm now of the belief that the way to support people is through active listening, not trying to be a problem-solver straight away.'

Michael's advice on listening without problem-solving

- Listening is important because it allows someone to express what's going on emotionally. How they're feeling at that given time is completely unique to them. No one else can feel exactly the way they do in that moment, and they should be allowed to express that and be listened to.

- When you're listening to a partner, rather than trying to give solutions – which is something I know I struggle with myself as a 'fixer' – a better response, even if you don't totally understand what they are feeling, could be to say 'I acknowledge that you feel stressed.' Tell them that's OK, and understandable. Then you can ask them to tell you more by saying, 'Tell me more about it – what you've got to do and why you think it's overwhelming.' Just that validation that how you feel is totally normal and OK takes a huge weight off.

- You don't always need to fix the situation. If someone tells you they are feeling worthless, the key to unlocking that is to say, 'Can you tell me why you feel like that?' Reaching out and admitting you're unwell and that you need help doesn't imply that you need a solution from that person.

- In a more day-to-day situation, you might use a little more prompting because you know the person and you know their behaviours, and what might have worked for them before. But let them make their own suggestions and plans to help themselves get through it, because it will help them feel like they're not a failure. By helping them plan what's going to work for them, you are allowing them to make their own decisions – and that is very empowering.

Leave your baggage outside the door

There are two steps involved in good listening. The first is that you leave your own perspective outside the room, so that you can stay with the other person's viewpoint. And the second is that you stay with the feelings, rather than moving into solution-finding. You need both these steps for people to really feel validated.

You have to start by meeting them where they are and trying to understand that first. For example, with depression, you have to put one foot in the black hole with them before you can bring in any shades of grey. You might be trying to guide the other person into a less black position, but that's not where you begin. You can't start by saying, 'Oh, life's not so bad,' because actually, first of all, you have to understand just how life in a black hole feels for that person.

I sometimes talk to people about being on one side of a wall. They're on their side, and you're on your side, shouting over the top of the wall. Just saying 'Hey, jump over! It's nice on this side!' isn't helpful – because if they could have jumped over, if they had any means of getting over the wall, they would have already done it. They can see it's nice on your side, all green grass and blue sky, and they know it's raining on their side and just grey and concreted over. Of course they want to get to your side – but they don't know how to. They might need your help to get over the wall. Sometimes, you might have to get a ladder, climb up, go over the wall, take the ladder with you, and climb down to meet the person where they are, on their side of the wall.

It's important to put yourself aside, to try and rein in your own reaction to what you are hearing, because what the person needs from you in that moment is for you to understand what it is like for them, to the best of your ability. There are certain situations where this is going to be hard, for example, for a parent. Parents might default straight

'True listening involves…
a setting aside of the self.'

M. Scott Peck

back into a pattern of dominance or control. They might say, 'I know you better than anyone, so therefore I know what's best for you. So let's do this, or try this.' Of course, most parents who see their child going through a hard time or in any sort of pain, will be desperate to change that fact. They will want to get it sorted as soon as possible. This is understandable, but it might not be helpful.

There is evidence to show that very careful self-disclosure, used in a relevant way and related to what you're hearing, can be helpful. A lot more therapy these days is about trying different routes to help people open up, perhaps asking the same question in a different way. We practise much more self-revealing now, for example: 'I'm thinking that this might have brought up something to do with your past, but I don't know if you agree with that.' This approach might help someone to pause and reflect on what it is they are feeling. Putting a short, neutral question out there might make them say, 'No, I'm not thinking that at all,' or 'Oh yes, I hadn't thought of that.' When you're talking with friends and family, there's no reason why you can't be a bit more open and exploratory. You're not a therapist. You're just someone that's there for them, because you care. By saying, for example, 'I had a recent bereavement, too, and what I noticed was how it affected everyone in my family quite differently,' you can make a connection with the person you're listening to through sharing, but without imposing. You're making yourself more human and approachable for someone that wants to talk, but you're not making it about you.

Good listening is about leaving your own baggage outside the door, which frees you up to be really present with the person in their space, as opposed to yours. And that means really holding back on your opinions and your solutions. It's then about going beyond what is superficially said, to unpack the layers of meaning behind a statement and encourage the person to elaborate on what they are saying.

The power in that listening experience is about validation. It's a feeling that someone has actually stepped over a line between you and them to stand alongside you momentarily. In order to achieve that, there are some things that you might have to stop yourself from doing – and that takes discipline.

In my work with mental health nurses, we try to teach them not to move straight into either finding a solution or refuting the experience of the patient. It's an impulse. If a patient is angry because they feel unfairly treated, the immediate response is to explain to them that they're not being unfairly treated. But that is the nurse's perspective, not the patient's, so by telling them that, you're invalidating what they are feeling in that moment. Or they might try and find a solution, saying to the patient, 'What's made you feel it was unfair? Let me solve it.' Instead, we try to teach them to stay with the feeling of unfairness and not to move away from it until that feeling dissipates.

It's a little bit like mindfulness in that you recognise the problem, then sit with it, but you don't actively do anything with it. Just realise and accept that it's there. See what happens when you sit with it. Acknowledge those feelings and don't try to hide from them or bury them. In taking this kind of 'feeling' approach to exploring what might be a problem, you experience the emotion of it before moving into a more cerebral, thinking arena.

Ask them about how they're feeling in order to help you to step away from your own position. If someone tells you they feel down, instead of thinking about what feeling down is like in your experience, you could say: 'You need to tell me what it feels like for you.' You might even say: 'My down and your down are going to be really different things. So let's leave my down out of this. Let's really understand your experience of down. Tell me some more and help me understand what it feels like to be you.'

You won't necessarily understand what it feels like for that person, because everyone's experiences are unique and different. You might often hear phrases like 'You've got no idea what I'm talking about' or 'You don't know what I'm going through'. And it's true. But there isn't a need for you to know what they're going through. What's important is to try and help them make sense of things and help explore their feelings.

If you suspect that a situation has gone beyond someone having a hard time and might have escalated into something more serious like self-harm, clinical depression or suicidal thoughts or feelings, you could do a bit of research. In a crisis situation, you should call the emergency services. But you can also educate yourself on signs and symptoms, research the topic and what kind of help might be available before things get that bad, or to help you spot the signs that something is really wrong and that the person needs further or urgent care. Learning about the issue can help prepare and work out how you might react. There is a list of helpful resources on pages 187–92 that can help with this. It's important that you don't respond with shock, or fear, or come across as disgusted or disapproving of what's being said. If you say to someone, 'Are you hurting yourself?' or, 'Have you thought you might not be able to carry on?' you are not going to make them go and do those things. It's not going to put ideas in their head. In fact, it can often be helpful for someone to realise that what they are thinking and feeling can be said out loud, and that can be the first step on the road to recovery.

Listening to a family member, loved one or partner who is going through a hard time can be enormously challenging. What's important is to keep communication going while someone is in the throes of distress and to focus on their viewpoint.

Jackie, clinical psychologist and Samaritans trustee

How to avoid trying to problem-solve for others

With family, a lot of factors come into play that can affect the nature of conversations. It's not that family members have an inability to listen to each other, but it frames the conversation in a different way if you've got a strong relationship with somebody. Often what happens in conversations with loved ones or people close to you, is that they don't think you're going to understand, or they don't want to be a burden or trouble you. Then, all of a sudden, they're at a point where it's hard for them to make that leap into very personal or emotional territory.

I was always such a problem-solver and, in many ways, I still am by instinct. But in the years since I've been a Samaritan, if friends or family have had a deeper, more meaningful discussion with me, I'm less inclined to try and give them advice and solve problems, and I'm more inclined to just listen to what they are saying.

As a Samaritan, you spend time building up a rapport with the caller and getting them to trust you. This can be hard, because you're just a voice on the end of the phone and often they are talking about a highly emotive subject. However, once we've built that trust, callers sometimes feel more able to talk to us than someone they know. Samaritans volunteers care about the person on the other end of the phone, but it's a conversation with somebody they've never met and will never speak to again. Time and time again, callers say: 'I can talk to you, but I couldn't talk to my mother/brother/whoever about this because I wouldn't want to burden them or worry them.'

When you have a conversation with a partner or a loved one, you know one another so you can just pick it up in a relatively normal way without having to build a rapport – but you can never detach yourself emotionally from your friends or family. And while Samaritans volunteers will never give advice or tell someone what to do, most of us, when talking to someone we are in a close personal relationship with, tend to dive in with a solution, saying things like: 'Why don't you do this?' Often, it's because we don't like seeing someone we love feel stressed or down.

But the problem with just leaping in with a solution is that you haven't really listened to what they're saying and so you haven't really understood where the person's coming from. The better you know somebody, the more in danger you are of making assumptions. You might think, 'Oh, I understand her, I know how she's feeling.' But it's likely that the person then won't feel listened to or validated, because you haven't allowed them the space to explore what's going on. They may not understand exactly why they're feeling like they're feeling, and they could just need space to get to the bottom of it, but you've taken that space away by jumping straight in with solutions and ideas. This approach can make them defensive, and they might then push back.

There is a place for probing a bit more in conversations with somebody you know well. As long as you lead with empathy and don't take control away from them, that can be OK. At Samaritans, we ask open questions to help someone think about what their options are, for example, 'What kind of help or support do you think might benefit you?', 'Are you talking to anybody about this?' or 'What distraction techniques do you use?' In a personal conversation, it's fine to suggest something similar, or at least to open them up for discussion. Just make sure you're phrasing them as questions rather than telling the person what to do.

It can be very difficult to hear a loved one talk about feeling worthless or being down on themselves, simply because it's likely that you'll have the opposite view. But by saying 'No, you're not worthless! You're amazing, you're wonderful!' – even though it's true – what you're telling that person is 'I disagree with you'. And for someone in a loop of negative self-talk, all they will hear is that you think they're wrong. The person might then stop telling you about what they're feeling because they can't connect or make you understand. That might leave you feeling despair and anxiety over your 'failure' to solve the problem, or worse, you might assume it's all fine now and that everything's sorted because they've stopped telling you about feeling bad. The danger then is that you're perpetually misunderstanding each other.

The instinct to try and nurture and protect on the part of the 'fixer' can be very strong. But often, someone going through a hard time won't quite realise that what they need is someone to just listen to them. So it's about reading the signs, responding, and offering a listening ear first and foremost.

Giles, Samaritans volunteer and trustee

'Most people do not listen with the intent to understand; they listen with the intent to reply.'

Dr Stephen R. Covey

Chapter 8:
Don't make it about you

Don't project your experience onto someone else

We tend to filter whatever we see, hear or feel through our own experiences. What was that like for me? Does that resonate with what I know to be true? We might use our own personal frame of reference to try and make sense of what the other person is saying, but that's not the same as knowing what the other person is going through – and hearing all about your own experiences might not be helpful for them.

It's natural that, in the usual rhythm and flow of a conversation between two people, you will share and say, 'Oh, yeah, me too.' It's OK to reference similar experiences to help someone explore their options for talking or getting additional support. Having a shared understanding can often be why someone approaches you for support in the first place. It can also help with starting a difficult conversation with someone you are worried about. By opening up about your own experience, you're showing that this is a safe space to discuss how they're feeling, too.

A little bit of self-disclosure implies empathy, but don't talk about yourself for too long – put yourself to one side for a minute, be present and ask about whether the other person can tell you a little more. Remember not to give your opinion on what they should try to do, unless they ask for it, and never tell someone what to think. It's important to make sure the conversation is focused on the person you're supporting. If you find that you're talking too much, you could ask them an open question to bring the conversation back to them.

They might not be quite ready to open up yet, but ask yourself: have you listened to what they are really telling you? Or have you gone too quickly to a connection with your own experiences? Have you made an assumption about what they might be feeling? Do you suddenly find yourself presuming that they feel the same way you feel about it? Everyone's emotions, responses and reactions will be different. The main thing is to focus on them, and let them talk, giving them room to express and explore whatever it is that they want to talk about. Focus on neutral territory so that you're not projecting your experience on to their situation.

How to recognise when you have stopped actively listening

There are certain red flags that indicate when you've stopped actively listening. If you hear yourself say any of the phrases listed below, it means you've closed down, and it's time to change direction.

- 'So, don't you think you should…'
- 'What about if you…'
- 'Perhaps you could try…'
- 'Why don't you…'
- 'If you could just…'
- 'I knew you were going to do/say that.'

If this happens, take a moment to pause, take a deep breath and then try asking an open question to bring the focus back to the person you're listening to.

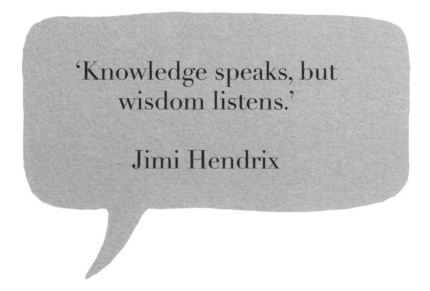

'Knowledge speaks, but wisdom listens.'

Jimi Hendrix

Avoid talking about yourself too much

When you're having a normal conversation and listening to somebody, you're often searching for those cues that will enable you to come in with your own anecdote. If somebody says, 'My dog died. I'm feeling really sad about it,' you might then offer, 'Yeah, I had a dog that died, too' – and then you might spend the next 20 minutes talking about your experience. While the other person may be interested, it hasn't actually given them the opportunity to talk about how they're feeling. That 'not really listening but waiting to make your own point' can be a habit that's hard to break. More useful is active listening, where you are really concentrating on what the other person is saying, not interrupting, and carefully considering the points they are making.

If someone insinuates that they want to talk, perhaps what they want is for you to say, 'Well, how are you feeling about that?' or 'How has that impacted on you?' That might allow the conversation to eventually evolve and become something different. Perhaps the dog dying has brought up feelings about a past experience of losing a family member, and this is their way – perhaps not even consciously – of introducing a difficult subject; testing the water. The thing a person in difficulty wants to talk about is very often not the thing that they mention first.

Silence can be really powerful. If somebody says, 'I had a bad day yesterday,' you can just let it hang in the air for a little bit. Or you could say something absolutely minimal, like 'Did you?' – in an encouraging way – to give them an opportunity to enlarge upon their initial statement. It indicates you're giving them permission to carry on. By not closing them down or making it about you, you haven't said, 'Gosh, this is awkward, I don't really want to talk about something bad.'

A lot of people are scared of discussing 'bad' things, thinking that talking about them might just encourage the other person to wallow in them, whereas that person may simply need to express their worry. Sometimes when fears are spoken out loud, they don't seem as awful as when they are swirling around inside your head. By giving that person the chance to share in a conversation that is focused on them and their feelings, you might be able to help them move past their fears or worries, or at least begin to understand them.

Anne, Samaritans volunteer

Even if you know someone well, you won't always know what they are thinking

The way we listen to each other in daily life is impacted by the other information that we have about the people we're talking to. Sometimes, during periods of conflict in our closer relationships, we might hear – or say – things like 'Did you even listen to what I just said?' or 'If you would just let me finish my sentence.' When you're engaging with someone close to you, you will know – or presume you know – their behavioural patterns, and so you might naturally anticipate or predict what they're going to say or what their reaction would be to certain things.

It might be the case that you approach tricky conversations presuming you already know what the other person will think, feel or say. But if you suspect they are stressed, anxious or depressed, you have to accept that you probably don't know what they are thinking. Remember to ask yourself, 'Am I actually hearing what they are saying?'

We've all experienced moments of frustration or anger in which it might feel like we're not being listened to at all, or that our conversations and interactions seem to be occurring in isolation, and we are unable to connect. We know that lack of connection can invoke annoyance, loneliness, make you feel misunderstood, or simply cause you to feel unheard.

So even if your assumptions about how the other person would react do turn out to be correct, rather than saying 'I knew you'd say that', try asking an open question instead. This will keep the conversation flowing.

Sometimes there is quite a slow descent into a situation where you might suddenly understand that someone is feeling a lot worse than you had initially realised, and keeping your assumptions to yourself can enable them to explore these feelings with you. Someone who started off by talking about feeling 'a bit down' might end up telling you that they're actually finding it really hard to cope. So ask them to explain it to you: ask them how they are feeling, and if it is different from normal. Ask them what that's like.

'There's a lot of difference between listening and hearing.'

G. K. Chesterton

Don't assume you know best

There seems to be a gap in the help that's available for people who reach out for support with their mental health. On one side, there are clinical mental health services. Here, the main concerns are symptoms, behaviours, traits, diagnosis, medicalised intervention and treatment, whether that's a 10-minute appointment with the GP followed by a waiting list to see a counsellor, or long-term inpatient care at a mental health facility. On the other side, you have well-meaning friends or family members. They operate from a place of love and concern, but are so desperate to prevent their loved ones from suffering that they often want to find a solution as quickly as possible. They tend towards dominance and control, trying to find ways to make everything better, which can be overwhelming and conflicting for the person in distress. This idea of 'I know best', and the accompanying desire to fix the situation and thereby control it, takes away the power from the person who is struggling. It can also inadvertently reaffirm their notion that they can't do it themselves.

But there's a space in between, where people want to have someone to stand alongside them and just be there while they go through whatever it is they're going through – not to find a solution, but to simply be there, beside them, for support. Samaritans is in this middle space, offering a place to go when people want to let off steam, release the burden of whatever it is they are carrying and be told that someone cares, without judgement, without pressure, with empathy and in confidence. Overwhelmingly, people just feel a need to be heard. To tell someone something and hear the words 'That's OK,' or 'I hear what you are saying.' Or 'Do you want to talk about it?' This in-between place is a place we can all get to, by discussing our feelings more openly and listening to one another more carefully.

Asking to be heard and asking for help are two different things

James Downs, 31, from Cardiff, first started struggling with OCD and eating disorders in his early teens. At school, he didn't have many close friendships, and at home, there was a sense that everything had to be OK because his mum had mental health problems, and he didn't want to be an extra burden on her.

For a long time, James felt isolated and lonely, as if his problems or emotions were unreachable by anybody else. And when he felt like he wasn't being listened to, he would give up and not bother to talk, which made matters worse.

'I've had periods in my life where I've felt that there was nobody to turn to,' he says. 'The longer you carry a problem on your own, the heavier it can get. But by talking about it, you realise that, actually, it's not as heavy as you thought. It just gives you a bit of rest from carrying it all by yourself. If I want to talk to somebody – a friend, a family member, somebody on the phone – I'm not saying "Fix this." I'm not asking for their opinion. What I'm saying is, "Can we just hold this together for a bit? I'm struggling to hold this thing and carry it around on my own. It's getting a bit much for me."

'Sometimes people want to immediately move on to saying, "OK, so what can we do about that?" The thing about being heard is that you don't want their opinion, otherwise you would have asked for help. Asking to be listened to is quite different to asking for help, and I think people really confuse the two. But asking to just talk to somebody and be heard isn't the same as saying "I'm in crisis mode and I know that I need to ask for help with this."'

James has found that, with his friends and family, people sometimes seem frightened of listening, because they fear that they might be required to act in a certain way or obliged to offer help. 'I hear this a lot from my friends. But I tell them that they don't need to offer help or give advice. Sometimes people are put off listening because they don't want to take on the burden of someone else's issues. They might feel like they don't have the capacity to get involved, which is totally understandable – we all have our own busy lives to deal with. I really try to reassure them that it's not as daunting as it might seem. It can be as simple as really paying attention to somebody, sitting there and listening. The expectation on you, in terms of action is very, very small. But it's still profoundly meaningful. It's not about worrying "What should I do or say? Am I going to do the right thing? Am I going to say the right thing? Will I make it worse?" Actually, you don't need to say very much at all, other than asking questions or giving responses that show you're engaged. Just listening is enough.'

Unfortunately, what kept James silent and stopped him from speaking out for so long was that he found talking to other people difficult and this made it harder for him to ask for help. 'In a healthcare setting, going to see a professional and trying to explain what was going on for me and that I was finding things really difficult was hard. I wanted someone to listen. And I think not feeling like someone understood made me withdraw. I was so vulnerable, and opening up was really painful.'

In general, James felt his experience was based on behaviour, symptoms and problem-solving in the form of a diagnosis: 'Because I had OCD and eating problems, all the treatments were really focused on behaviour change, to fix the symptoms and then get you out of the system. There's a fundamental difference between someone analysing my behaviours and working out what's going on so that we can fix it, and just being spoken to with compassion and empathy. The latter can do a lot of good.'

As his mental health got worse, James began to feel as though his problems weren't real. 'That pushed me into some psychologically dark places. I felt like I had anxiety or emotional pain that I struggled to cope with alone, but when I did try and share it, people would run away from it. As a result, I ended up going down a really pathological route of psychiatric problems. But looking back, I was just a young person who was struggling to cope with life and relate to the world. I just felt very, very lonely and I didn't have anyone to sit with that feeling with me.'

When his eating problems got really bad, James had to stop going to school because he wasn't well enough to attend. He received care at home as an outpatient, from a community intensive treatment team. When he went on to university at age 20, he found the change difficult. 'I got so unwell in the first term, I stopped going to lectures or even going out at all. I ended up having to take the rest of the year off. I tried to go back the following year and it didn't work again. I remember feeling extremely isolated. I felt lonely and it was hard. For most of that year I didn't really go to classes or lectures. I didn't see anyone, not even the people in my house.'

Due to long waiting lists and some admin issues with transferring medical information from his home to his university town, James was unable to access the specialist eating disorder support and treatment that he desperately needed. 'I completely gave up on trying to reach out to people until it became dangerous for my physical health. I really bought into the idea that it didn't matter if I was struggling because nobody cared.'

James found himself living in a shared house where, instead of attending his university lectures and getting to know people, he was hiding away, with his eating disorder getting worse and worse until he ended up feeling suicidal. 'I felt like I just couldn't exist with it on my own. I couldn't exist at the same time as feeling such unbearable pain. And there were moments, the most terrifying moments, where I felt there was just nowhere to go. I felt totally alone.'

James went to the GP and told her he had plans to take his own life, but he didn't get the help he needed. 'I went away thinking that there was nothing left. And so I tried to kill myself. I can't really remember what happened, but somewhere in the middle of it all, I called Samaritans. After that I don't really remember very much, apart from waking up in hospital. When I got back to my room, the door had been broken down and I'd written the Samaritans number on my table. I remember feeling so relieved. I called a few more times after I came out of the hospital. There was one call, when I got back home, when the person on the end of the line said something like, "That sounds like a really hard time. That sounds really difficult." I don't remember exactly what she said, but I remember exactly how it made me feel. I felt like it was reasonable that I had found the experience difficult. And that was the first time I'd felt that. It was like a revelation. It was such a relief, to realise that anybody would find that difficult. It wasn't just me. It wasn't that I was a bad person, or that I was weak because I couldn't cope with my feelings. That was the start of a really long process of trying to actually work through everything, and realising that it was worth getting help.'

James left university, went back home and got the specialist eating disorder treatment he needed, more than six years after being first diagnosed with severe anorexia. 'It's been a really long process, but I could have given up completely.'

In his experience, the value of being listened to came down to a sense of validation. Someone saying, 'It's absolutely normal that you would feel this way,' and 'There's nothing wrong with whatever it is that you're going through,' really changed how he saw himself. Before that, he always felt like his behaviour and his feelings weren't reasonable. 'At my worst, I felt like what I was going through wasn't real because I was so alone with it,' he says. 'That, alongside being very malnourished, meant I lost touch with reality. It was scary. But when you reach out and you get a response that is about getting fixed, it tells you that you're not worth listening to. The power of somebody who can just sit with what you're saying and recognise that what you're going through is real to you is profoundly connecting because it makes you feel valid.'

Over time, James has become more and more able to cope in different situations – both with professionals and with other people in his life – and is able to confidently show the parts of him that aren't OK all the time. He returned to studying and now has a master's degree in psychology and education from the University of Cambridge. He has developed meaningful relationships with people who love him the way he is and has accepted that he doesn't need to be perfect all the time.

'Listening is something that has really helped me through some dark moments. It hasn't been about the person being skilled, or offering exactly the right response, or trying to fix anything or give advice. It's about the amount that they've paid attention, and the way they've shown empathy and compassion. Just being there and giving someone your time is one of the greatest gifts that you can give somebody.'

James's advice on being a better listener

- Please be reassured that you do not need to fix everything. You don't need to come up with solutions or figure out a plan. You don't even have to say very much at all to make someone feel really listened to. Just let them know they're not on their own with it.

- Try not to be too confrontational. Try to ask for the space to have a good conversation by saying that it's important to you, you want to be there for them, and it would be great to talk it through. If now's not a great time, when would it be good?

- It's really not about being a specialist or having particular knowledge. It's about being a compassionate human being. I wish people had the confidence to realise they are able to offer real help just by listening.

- Instead of getting caught up in the details of how you are responding or wondering what the best response or the right thing to say might be, focus on connecting with that person and helping them feel safe. If you give an imperfect response, it doesn't matter. The person you are talking to will forgive you, because they will know that your intentions are good, and you are trying your best.

- Making a connection with someone helps them find a level of safety and accepting what they say in that safe space is so validating. It's really helpful when somebody can see what you're going through, accept it for what it is and not want to change it.

Don't tell someone how to feel

It can be hard to see someone you care about lose interest in their life, especially if it is one you share. Trying to get someone to focus on the positive may seem like a helpful thing to do if they are feeling bad about themselves or their situation, but often this is not something that is helpful to hear. It can sound like you're telling the person that their feelings are wrong, or that you don't believe them, even if your intentions are very different. Telling someone to 'look on the bright side' or saying 'Cheer up, it could be worse,' can exacerbate feelings of guilt at not being able to enjoy the good things in their life, which someone suffering from poor mental health might already be struggling with.

Try and avoid the following unhelpful phrases:

- 'Cheer up.'
- 'You don't have anything to be sad/worried about.'
- 'Look at everything you have – you have so many reasons to be happy.'
- 'You're so much better off than others.'
- 'It could be worse.'
- 'It's not the end of the world.'
- 'You are strong.'
- 'Just get on with it.'
- 'You're the only one who can change how you're feeling.'
- 'You need to snap out of it and pull yourself together.'

Coping statements

Even though it is difficult to see someone you love or care about in pain and not be able to do anything about it, try to encourage them to take control in a way that feels supportive rather than judgemental. Overleaf are some coping statements or affirmations that you could share with the person you're supporting to remind them that they can either accept or change what they are feeling. Learning to accept something takes practice, but if someone can identify what's troubling them, they can repeat these affirmations to help them feel like they have the power to alter their own mindset.

• This is upsetting, but the feeling will pass eventually.
• I don't have to let this bother me.
• I've felt this way before, and I'm still here.

Listen without judgement

One of the key components of a Samaritans conversation is listening without judgement. You don't want the person you're talking to to be afraid of prejudice or rejection. So be careful what you say and how you physically react. Samaritans volunteers are trained to remain neutral, emotionally impassive and controlled in their reactions: to put their own opinions and reactions to one side so that they are removed enough from the situation to provide a calm response. This is obviously a lot harder for friends, family members and loved ones, as when you see someone you care about suffering, it makes you suffer, too, so being able to keep a lid on your feelings is less likely. But what's important is to put the person who's in distress or who's having a hard time first. If you need to do the same for yourself at another time, then that's fine; there's time for that. But right then, in that moment, try to give the floor to the person that's being asked to be heard.

If you are concerned that the level of emotion might escalate quickly, don't worry. It's OK to cry. That's a valid response and it shows you care. It's healthy to have a natural emotional response, particularly in reaction to something that's very difficult to hear. Expressing emotions and crying together isn't a bad thing. We're all human beings, and if you care about someone, it's OK to let it show. It's important not to suppress your feelings, and it might be helpful to demonstrate to the other person how you feel. But make sure you are as prepared as possible for those emotions to surface, and think beforehand about how you can react in the most helpful way so that you don't put the person off speaking further. If you get very upset or react in an intense, confrontational way, it is likely to push them away, leaving them confused about where to turn to next, and wondering whether they should speak to anyone else at all.

Keep the focus on them and try to keep the conversation calm enough so that they're not scared to share anything else. Even if you are overwhelmed on the inside, pause, take a big breath and try to contain any emotionally explosive reactions such as anger or frustration. The most helpful thing you can do when someone discloses something difficult is to accept what they are saying and try to understand their point of view.

If you don't get anywhere with that first try, come back again, once the emotions have settled, and give it another go. Just keep talking. It might be enough to give someone a hug and let them know that you are there for them. They might not be ready to talk yet – you can't force someone to open up – but by letting them know you are there to listen, you might alter their state of mind enough for them to be able to open up in a day or two.

PART THREE

Practical Support and Self-Care

'It's not what happens to you but how you react to it that matters.'

Epictetus

Chapter 9:
Practical ways to help

Research and preparation can really help

One of the ways you can get ready for a difficult conversation with someone you're worried about is to prepare yourself to hear something you might find upsetting. If you suspect that a family member, a friend or a partner is having a hard time and you want to talk with them, take time to think about how they might react – and what your own reaction to what they tell you might be.

Running through the questions you want to ask and the possible outcomes – either in your head, on paper or with someone else you trust – will help you to avoid reacting impulsively. It is a huge compliment for someone to trust you enough to confide in you, and you can repay that by responding with sensitivity. Reacting negatively may make the person you're listening to feel worse or stop them from asking for help in the future.

Be aware of how times of change in people's lives can exacerbate mental health issues – this includes things like divorce, grief, moving house or going away to university. Use these moments to check in with people and have good conversations about what they might experience at these times.

Research and read up on the different kinds of mental ill health that can affect anybody at any time, from low mood and anxiety to depression and bipolar. By preparing yourself, you will feel more able to respond to what someone might say without experiencing panic and distress of your own.

Whatever situation the person you are supporting is going through, there will be trusted information available. So find out more about what they're experiencing – it could help you think of other ways in which you could support them. By doing some research of your own, you can feel more informed when helping them explore their options, and it may take some of the pressure off them having to explain everything to you.

Making a safety plan

Pooky Knightsmith is an educator specialising in child and adolescent mental health. She is autistic and has a history of eating disorders, anxiety, depression and PTSD. At times, these issues have collided to make life very difficult and she has found herself unable to manage alone. 'About five years ago, things just dramatically unravelled,' she says. 'I ended up actively suicidal at various points, and spent time at The May Tree suicide respite centre and in hospital for inpatient care with anorexia.'

During this time, thoughts of suicide and self-harm were at the forefront of Pooky's mind all the time, and she was constantly in a place of extreme emotional pain. 'I was really, really low, and so anxious that I went through periods of not being able to leave the house. And when I did, I was having multiple panic attacks and a lot of dissociation. One of the things that helped me was being able to pick up the phone to someone who would either talk to me or listen, depending on where I was at. If it was earlier in the evening, I would talk to my friend Joe, but if it was the middle of the night, then Samaritans always felt like the only option. I found that having someone on the other end of the phone could help me stay connected with the world so that I wouldn't completely dissociate. I would stay more present and be able to problem-solve. Having someone who can listen to that pain and not run away from it was really important. It would be just enough to stop me from doing myself any harm.'

Pooky found the support of her friend Joe invaluable at these times; sometimes he would support her to get treatment, sometimes they would talk and sometimes he would just be there. 'He would both metaphorically and literally pick me up when I was down, or sit with me while I cried – often in really public places – but he never let any of that bother him. He would just sit there with it. He just let the emotion happen.'

In Pooky's experience, doing some research and planning what you want to say before you go to the GP can help you get a more helpful response. 'Unfortunately, not all GPs are experts in mental health, and often they are overworked. The difficult thing is that if you do get pushback from a GP, that often feeds into a lot of negative self-narrative that's going on about being undeserving of help, and it can really shut the door on further treatment. What I advise people to do is do a bit of research, such as making sure you book an appointment with the best person at the surgery. Try calling up in advance and asking if there is someone who specialises in mental health.' She also recommends taking a friend and having someone there to advocate for you, whether they come into the consulting room with you or are just there to support you leading up to the appointment. 'You've got a really short amount of time to speak to your GP, so planning what information you need to convey and what you might want to happen next can help.'

Being referred to a specialist is important, as the right diagnosis will lead to the right care and treatment. 'It's really important to try and treat everyone as a human being and to look beyond labels – to look for strength rather than challenge. However, we do live in an age where there is good research and as soon as I was given the correct diagnosis, overnight my treatment was able to change and adapt based on what was actually wrong with me. With complex PTSD, I was able to access Eye Movement Desensitisation and Reprocessing (EMDR) therapy – an interactive psychotherapy technique – and in a matter of months, problems that had blighted my life and controlled my emotions and feelings for decades became much more manageable. Likewise, having the right kind of medication gave me a platform from which I could begin to live.'

For many years, Pooky avoided medication due to the stigma associated with it and the feeling that she should be able to manage on her own. 'But once I did start taking medication, it was an absolute game-changer for me: first in terms of being able to reduce my anxiety enough to eat, but also for more specific PTSD symptoms. It didn't mean that everything was suddenly OK overnight, it just meant I was beginning at a slightly better starting point. Sometimes people are critical about medication, but there's no shame involved. If you're a diabetic, you would take insulin. So why are antidepressants any different?'

Pooky is a big advocate of safety plans. 'If you're worried about a friend, being brave enough to say, "Let's talk about this and think about how we can keep you safe," can really help. You can ask questions like: "What are the items that we should be trying to keep away from you? Are there places that you shouldn't go? When you're in absolute crisis mode and vulnerable to doing something impulsive, what is something you could do in the first minute to keep yourself safe?" It might be as simple as saying "I'm going to force myself to play a game on my phone for one minute and see how I feel after that." These really basic things can help. The other thing about safety planning is that it gives you a framework for a difficult discussion. You can find template safety plans at stayingsafe.net – you can either download a PDF, or you can create one with your own questions. A safety plan can be so helpful because when someone is at crisis point, they can't access the logical thinking part of the brain, but if you've got a plan that you've printed out, and you're carrying it with you, or you've got it on your phone, then you just follow a set of instructions that you wrote for yourself in a time of calmness. It's important to think about that crisis point during times when you do feel more well or in control. Because when you're in the middle of a crisis, you're literally trying to get through it minute by minute.'

For Pooky, having this kind of plan has helped a lot, and having a friend be there to understand what's going on has been really important at times when she has felt despairing and worthless. 'Just knowing that there is someone by my side, who cares enough to listen, regardless of quite how broken I might be, who isn't scared by the things that are scaring me, makes me feel validated and gives me hope.'

How you can offer practical support

Sometimes, the only thing you can do for someone who is going through a hard time emotionally is help out with practical tasks like cooking and washing. It might take time for someone to be able to vocalise what they are going through. Often, when someone is really suffering emotionally, they might feel like it doesn't matter what you say – that in that moment, nothing can make them feel better. At these times, just being there is what counts. When that person is ready, they will open up.

So when someone is going through a difficult time, you could try helping them with practical tasks to help take some of the weight off their shoulders. This could include:

• helping buy and prepare food;

• sorting out bills for them;

• helping them get dressed;

• offering them a lift somewhere;

• looking after their pet;

• helping out with household chores;

• helping out with other practical tasks.

Keeping on top of the practical things that need to be done day-to-day can stop many people from feeling overwhelmed and anxious.

To-do list

Use this space to write notes for a possible to-do list that might help someone who is struggling.

1 Make a list (if this is the first thing you write down, you will always have something to tick off)

2 ....

3 ....

4 ....

5 ....

6 ....

7 ....

8 ....

9 ....

10 ....

Practical activities

Remind the person you are supporting that there are certain activities which can be used as coping mechanisms. You could help them create a plan or record of doing them. Here are some ideas.

Practise kindness towards others
- Take unneeded items to a charity shop.
- Recommend something you love to someone.
- Visit an elderly neighbour.
- Explore volunteering opportunities.
- Help someone with a project they are working on.

Creativity
- Cook or bake something challenging.
- Draw or paint something.
- Do a puzzle.
- Try writing a poem or a short story.
- Do some journalling or scrapbooking.
- Try an online craft tutorial.

Learn
- Do some research on something that interests you.
- Start learning a new language.
- Watch an interesting documentary.
- Read a book.
- Discover local history.

Exercise
- Go swimming.
- Ride a bike.
- Go for a short walk.
- Take an exercise class.
- Do an online fitness tutorial at home.

Hygiene and order
• Declutter your living space.
• Write a shopping list for the week.
• Change your bedclothes.
• Do some laundry.
• Organise your shelves.

Have a change of scene
• Visit a local beauty spot.
• Sit in a garden or park.
• Go for a drive.
• Walk to the shops.

Practise kindness towards yourself
• Mcditate.
• Do an online yoga tutorial.
• Put on your most comfortable clothes.
• Make yourself a cup of tea.

Human connection
• Arrange to see a friend.
• Find a club, team or community group that appeals to you.
• Call a family member.

Entertainment
• Go to the cinema or theatre.
• Make a themed playlist.
• Watch your favourite TV show.
• Listen to some new music.

Engage the senses
• Light a scented candle.
• Take a warm bubble bath.
• Wrap up in a cosy blanket.

Putting it into words

Hussain Manawer is a poet and activist who uses performance to process his experience of grief and issues around mental health.

'My journey through grief has been long and winding,' he says. 'I've lost a lot of people. But when I was 26 years old, my mum passed away, instantly and unexpectedly from a sudden brain aneurysm. It was like the pillar in my life had been removed. The foundation of the house became shaky, like I was on uneven ground. I felt like my life had been reset. The process of grief was, and still is, exceptionally hard.'

When his mum died, Hussain went into project-manager mode with his siblings, organising the funeral and sorting things out around the house. But a few days afterwards, it really hit him that she wasn't coming back. 'At this point, I still hadn't cried. But after the funeral, there were people in her house, going up her stairs, using the cutlery from her special drawer that no one ever opened but her. I suddenly knew that she wasn't there anymore. I just burst into tears – I realised we had lost her.'

People handle their grief differently. 'The grieving process is a bespoke, unique experience tailored and designed for you. But you can handle it and you can get through it because that's exactly what your loved one would want for you. If I get to heaven and tell my mum all I've done is sat around crying, she'd say "Where are my grandkids? What about your job? I raised you better than that."

'A big thing in Asian culture is weddings, and I said to my sister just before she got married, "This is going to be really hard for you because Mum won't be there." And she said, "No, it's not – Mum did it without her dad being there." And that put a lot into perspective for me, because our mum lost her dad when she was young, too. She managed to get through her entire life without him. She was a living, breathing example of living with the loss of a parent.'

Hussain found that sometimes people didn't know what to say, perhaps due to inexperience or fear of their own trauma surfacing. 'In a way, I became very reclusive. I found myself speaking more to people who had lost someone. It was like I needed to find people who had the right words. When you talk to someone who has been through something similar, they make the space for you to say what you need to say, how you need to say it, without worrying you shouldn't be feeling the way you do, or that you're holding on to it for too long. I gravitated towards people who had lost someone themselves and survived it. It was like I needed to see the outcome.'

At his mum's funeral, Hussain spoke to a friend who had lost his dad, and remembers him saying that it would be the worst day of his life. 'I found that so hard, because up until this point everyone had been telling me "It's going to be alright, you're going to get through this," and all that. But he told the truth. And then he said, "What's good about it being the worst is that it can only get better." And he was right.

'It's so, so important to talk about your feelings and put a name to them because it helps you process what you're going through. These conversations and subjects are only now being talked about openly and freely. I started talking about mental health about nine years ago and a lot of people looked at me like, "Oh my word, stay away from him, you don't want to do that." But now more people are realising the damaging effects of not speaking out. The saddest thing is that a lot of people feel like they have no one to speak to.'

If Hussain doesn't express himself, he finds his internal monologue begins to suffer: 'My thoughts will fester into something horrible – into stress, into anger, into self-destruction and ultimately into oblivion, like a dark hole. It's like, internally, mentally, I'm thinking and thinking, but I'm smiling to everyone around me. But not saying how you feel can be really damaging and self-sabotaging. You have to find ways to express yourself otherwise it will eat you.'

This is where poetry comes in for Hussain. 'It's really important to me to actually put words to what I'm feeling – to try and name feelings or process through writing what I'm thinking. My brain is like a bunch of tangled wire. But when I write, it's like I can grab one of the wires and ease it out and I can overcome the confusion that was once there and things make a little bit more sense. Sometimes I just write and it's freestyle and the words just come, and I'm following the pen and the paper, and other times it's more metaphorical and I will spend a lot more time disguising certain things and making sure that the audience goes on a little journey to discover something themselves. When I'm writing, I'm always really vulnerable, but it has created a safe space for me to express myself in.'

Hussain had a friend he would call who lived in Australia. As they weren't face to face, he found it much easier to converse. 'It was so much easier for me that we couldn't see each other. He could just chat to me and give me a little bit of perspective. Even if he just said, "That must be hard." That's a really nice thing to hear sometimes: that someone else wants to acknowledge your struggle, your trauma, your daily battles.'

Hussain felt as though telling his loved ones what he was going through might scare or worry them. 'That's why it's good to go and see a therapist. A lot of people are looking for an answer they want to hear, not the truth: to be told that it's alright, rather than what you're doing is self-destructive and you need to make a change or you're going to ruin your life. I called Samaritans and I went to three therapists. The thing that helped me most was cognitive behavioural therapy, where I learned about my behaviour patterns and triggers. It was definitely hard. I'd never known anyone else in my life who'd gone to therapy before. I'd never known anyone from a Pakistani background pay to go and see a middle-class white lady in central London. It all seemed very, very obscure, until I realised that she was a professional, there to help. And when I learned to ask for help, life became a lot better.'

Hussain now finds that conversations with his friends are like therapy. 'They ask questions that are designed to fit around the emotion you're feeling. It's like combining their life experience with a kind of emotional activation, where they might say: "So, when you said this, did you meant that? Did you ever feel like that again? Or did you ever think this could have been because of that?" It's like an ability to identify and shine a magnifying glass on something that I'm living with, but I just can't see. Listening is important because it's like an invaluable currency that can't be used anywhere else but there and then. It's an enriching experience and one that can save lives.'

Helping someone make sense of what they are feeling

Everyone talks about the need for good communication, whether in relationships, organisations or governments – it's vital for every aspect of our daily lives. We're taught how to broadcast and how to present ourselves, but we're never actually taught how to listen. If I think back to school, university or work, I never ever had any kind of structured learning on how to listen, and yet it's an absolutely vital skill.

A good listener is someone who shows they care. It's someone who shows empathy and patience. Good listening is about having an authentic connection with someone and actively demonstrating that you are interested in the person you are listening to. Hearing is a physical act, but listening is processing what you've heard. It's understanding – or trying to understand – the context.

There are so many parts of the Samaritans active listening model that could really help others learn to listen better. It is possible to transpose the idea over, if we realise the importance of letting go of judgement. We might think we know what other people are thinking, or how they're going to react to various situations, particularly if we know them well, but we're not mind readers. It's important to let our friends, family members and colleagues know that they can talk and let it all out. It can really help people work out what's going on for them. What's important is getting alongside somebody and really listening with empathy. Some healthy challenge can be helpful, too, as long as you ensure you aren't coming across as judgemental. But honesty is really important in our interactions and communication.

One of the techniques we use at Samaritans is clarifying – offering back to the speaker what you have understood them to have said, to check what you think you've heard is correct. It gives the person a chance to reflect or correct. We often don't do that with close family and friends, but it can be beneficial, because it gives us a chance to understand a bit more, and it gives them the opportunity to say, 'Well, no, I'm not saying that at all.'

On a Samaritans call, through clarifying and careful questioning, I can ask someone, 'How long have you felt like this?' They might tell me, 'Oh, I've lived with this for years and years.' And so then I can ask: 'When you were at your lowest point in the past, what did you do that helped?' I can go on to ask if they think that might work now, and so on. You can gently prompt someone, and remind them that they have the power, the skills and knowledge to show up for themselves. Usually people do know exactly what they should be doing. If they tell you all the things that could work for them, you can say 'What do you think is stopping you from doing that again?' It's about passing the power back and ensuring that, even when people feel they are at their lowest ebb, they are given a bit of encouragement, praise and positive feedback.

Revealing and putting a name on those emotions – anger, sadness, fear, hope, jealousy, despair and so on – can be a huge relief. It can then give you clues that lead to what the person is most worried about. Naming our emotions is really important. Imagine a 'feelings index': pages and pages of feelings that you are able to pick and choose from, so that you can say, 'I feel sad, I feel angry, I feel betrayed or rejected.' We're not very used to working with emotional literacy. We are told that we have to suck it up, deal with it and move on. But naming our emotions and being honest with them encourages the kind of safe space where someone might then be able to help someone describe why they are feeling what they are feeling. That might mean that, as a parent, friend or partner, you will have to hear some really difficult truths. So remember that you also have to think about your own health. It's not going to help if you scream back at the person, but if you can, listen to what is happening, hear their emotions, feel the pain of it, and then, if you need to, you can go and talk to somebody else about how you feel.

One of the most important things about listening and giving the power back is the idea of introducing hope. Hope is such an important thing. It goes along with the aspiration and belief that someone is going to get through this rough patch. We really try to empower people through the Samaritans service, which is why we want people to name the emotion and express how they are feeling. It's much harder to do that than swooping in and rescuing someone, but it is so much more impactful if you can, because then that person has chosen their course. And you've been a supporter, a facilitator, a helper, but you're not one that has taken the responsibility of rescuing someone – because they've done that themselves.

Ruth has been a Samaritans volunteer since 2016 and was CEO of Samaritans from 2015 to 2020.

Naming feelings

How to help someone clarify what they are going through

It's important to give the person you're supporting lots of opportunities to explain how they're feeling and what they're going through. If you've ever tried to describe exactly how you're feeling, you'll know it's very hard to communicate it in a way that others understand, especially if you're talking about it for the first time. Often people will gloss over the important feelings, either because they don't know how to put how they feel into words, or because they feel embarrassed or ashamed.

One practical way of helping them with this is by asking clarifying questions like:

• 'When you say… do you mean… ?'
• 'What do you really mean by that?'
• 'It sounds like… is that how you feel?'

It can also be helpful to repeat back what someone has said to you so you can make sure you're understanding clearly. Clarifying questions and statements can help you, as the listener, try to understand better what the person you're talking to might be going through. It also gives them more opportunity to talk. We all use different words in conversation to explain things, so just be aware that someone else might talk about things differently or use different language, and if you don't get it at first, that's OK. To help you understand better, reflect what they say back to them and check that you've understood what they mean.

Putting a name to it

The ability to understand, name and express our emotions is important. Use these exercises to help others identify what they are experiencing so that they can verbalise and process their thoughts and feelings. Putting a name to what someone is feeling can often help them to open up about what they might be thinking.

Have a look at the words and phrases below and see if they recognise or identify with any of these feelings.

afraid	frustrated	on edge
amused	happy	overwhelmed
angry	hopeful	panicked
anxious	hopeless	peaceful
apathetic	humiliated	regretful
bored	joyful	satisfied
content	left out	stressed
defeated	like I don't fit in	stuck
disappointed	like I'm a burden	tense
disconnected	lonely	thankful
down	lost	trapped
energised	neutral	I don't know

Do they sometimes, often or rarely experience any of the physical sensations below?

aching muscles	feeling really tired	racing heartbeat
back pain	feeling sick	restlessness
churning stomach	grinding teeth	stress
digestive issues	headache	sweating
faster breathing	pins and needles	trouble sleeping

How would they rate their level of emotional wellbeing on a scale between 1 (I'm fine) and 10 (I'm in crisis)?

1   2   3   4   5   6   7   8   9   10

Ask the person you're listening to to write down why they think they might be feeling this way, or if there's anything else they would like to share.

_____

_____

_____

_____

_____

_____

_____

Chapter 10:
Accept it's OK to not be OK

Relinquish control and let people make their own decisions

The care and concern from friends and family who want to help comes from a good, protective place of love and wanting the best for someone. It is hard to see a friend, partner, sibling or colleague suffer. But relinquishing control is key.

Listening well can help keep the power with the person you're trying to help. You might want to say: 'Why don't you get up and go for a run? That will make you feel better!' But that's your path, your fix, your solution. It's not necessarily theirs. It might not help them at all. What happens if they go for a run and they hate it? They will come back and say, 'Why did you make me do that? Now my feet hurt.' And they'll still have a problem, but now they will also feel cross with you. Even if it feels hard, you must let the person you're trying to help own their feelings and their pain so that they can, at some point, control them. Give them the power of owning their decisions, their ideas and their process. It's their journey.

Deciding what someone else should do takes away their control and reinforces the idea that they aren't capable enough of making a good choice or decision for themselves. Telling someone, whether overtly or inadvertently, 'I'm going to do this for you. I'm going to tell you what I think you should do' is very invalidating and can do more harm than good. It goes back to the difference between someone asking for help and asking to be heard. If someone is saying 'I can't do this, I need help,' then of course you can take immediate steps towards practical solutions like protection, care, going to the GP, or whatever that situation needs. But if someone is saying 'I just want to talk, I just want to let it all out so that I can take a weight off,' then your place is to give them the floor. Show you care, and simply listen to what they have to say.

Let someone choose their own path

Darran, 39, from Bolton, had his first drink aged 16. By the end of his 17th year, he was a registered alcoholic. Over the course of the next 18 years, Darran's drinking got so bad that he lost his partner, his job and his home. A period of homelessness led to a suicide attempt and a nervous breakdown. Darran gave up drinking in 2015 and has been sober for four-and-a-half years. He is now a Samaritans volunteer and is studying Criminological and Forensic Psychology at university.

For Darran, drinking and depression went hand in hand. 'The deeper I got into it, the less I wanted to remember it, because of all the stupid stuff I'd done,' he says. 'It was a vicious circle. I was depressed anyway, and I think I just exacerbated that fact with drinking. I wasn't happy. I had been in relationships that I drove into the ground by the way I was acting. Everything I had, I messed up. It was a drama every day.'

It can be hard for families and loved ones to know what to do in a situation like the one Darran was in, but looking back, he's not sure there's anything anyone could have done or any advice that would have changed his behaviour. 'I think the main problem is love. If someone can see you are suffering and they care about you, they might go straight in and say, "I know what you need to make this better." And it's usually because they love you so much. Sometimes they want you to get better more than you want to get better yourself. My mum always used to say to me, "Give up the alcohol," or "Don't do this or that," and I didn't really want to hear it, to be honest. I didn't care about anything when I was at my worst.'

'I just needed someone to be there. I just needed support. It's not so much stopping someone doing something. It's being there when it does happen. It's being there to pick up the pieces. My mum must have known loads of times that I was either making a mistake or something was going to go wrong. But she very rarely used to put me down for it. She waited for something to happen and then she picked me up. And that's what kept us so close. There's nothing worse than someone saying "I told you so."'

Darran found himself stuck in a vicious cycle where he'd have bouts of abstinence and be alright for a while. But then he would start going out again, and weekend drinks with friends would turn into a daily event that would keep building up. 'I'd go on a wild bender, then do something stupid or try and kill myself. I'd be picked up, I'd go to rehab or hospital or home detox. And that's the way it went. But the time in between being alright and being at my worst was getting shorter, and I was just constantly on the edge of something bad happening. What I thought made me sociable was making me twice as antisocial. Towards the end, it was just a nightmare. I was lucky I got into rehab when I did, because otherwise I'd probably be dead.'

Over the years, Darran had a key worker with the alcohol services, and tried home detoxes and hospital detoxes – but he wasn't dealing with the root of his issues. 'I didn't really want to be there; I just needed to get it out of the way when my mum, my girlfriend or work was on my case, and I had to be seen to be doing something.'

Things got progressively worse in his thirties. 'I knew I didn't have long left the way I was carrying on, that it was going to end up badly somehow. There was one week where I had put myself in hospital three times. I was out of my mind. I had lost my job after getting done for drink-driving. My partner kicked me out. I went to my mum and said, "I've got nowhere to live," and she said, "You're not coming to live here." And that was a real turning point. Before then, no matter what state I was in or how bad it was, I could always guarantee that if I went to her with the big puppy dog eyes, she'd lay it on me for a bit and then she'd take my side. She knew I had nothing, but she basically had to just turn me around on the doorstep. I can't imagine how difficult it was for her to do that. I remember looking at her, looking at her face and looking at her eyes, and I could see the pain she was in. But I'll thank her for evermore for doing that, because it's exactly what I needed.'

Although Darran was used to having a chaotic life, being homeless was a completely different kind of chaos. 'It was terrible. I was on the go all the time. I ended up in an emergency shelter. It was manic, with fighting, shouting and loud music: constant pandemonium. Mentally, it was a really, really difficult place to be and I couldn't cope. I got taken out of there in an ambulance because I just didn't see any other way out.'

Darran woke up in hospital three days later, shivering due to detox, with his mum at the foot of his bed. She took him back in, but said she had plans to go away the following week, and asked if she could trust him to stay in the house on his own. 'Unfortunately, rather than seeing that she was trying to help me, I saw it as an opportunity to get a last drink in. She came back on the Monday and saw that I had drunk the house dry. When I woke up the next morning, it was like I had had a nervous breakdown. It was like something had switched in my brain. I just couldn't do it anymore. I couldn't look anyone in the eye. I couldn't leave my room. I felt this terrible, terrible guilt. After that, it got really bad. It got to the stage where I couldn't go out on my own. My mum would have to chaperone me everywhere and I couldn't do anything alone because I would have panic attacks.

'I got a new alcohol worker who put the challenge back on to me. She'd ask me, "Did you listen to what you've just said?" or "So, what are you going to do about it?" She used to listen to a lot of what I was saying and pick bits out to say back to me, and kind of challenge me on the truth of them, which made me really think about what it was that I was feeling. She'd say "Is that what really happened?" or "Was that really the case, do you think?" She had this ability to pick up on the right stuff, ask the right questions, and ask me about what I wasn't saying. I realised that she was listening to me as much as I listened to her. Previously, I had thought, No one wants to know the real me, no one wants to listen to me. She validated the fact that I was capable of being a better version of myself and that was who she wanted to see. I realised that if I wanted to do this properly, I would have to go to rehab.'

So Darran signed up for nine months of residential care. At first, it wasn't easy. 'It was mayhem. Total chaos. There were 36 addicts all shoved in a house together. I was completely out of my comfort zone and it was either sink or swim. And I sank – a lot. I said I was going home every day for the first month. But I learned to sit with all those people, all those addicts, and I learned to listen to them. All I used to do was listen to myself. I used to miss a lot of what people were really saying. I learned in there that I was able to just sit there with someone and talk, and find a kind of wavelength. Before that point, I used to listen for stuff I could use – something that would give me a little head start or excuse to get back to drinking.'

Three months into rehab, Darran learned that he could use the skill of listening for something else – to heal himself. 'I had a switch in my mindset of why I was actually doing what I was doing. I began to challenge and question myself. And when I learned to put some good intentions with that, I realised how important listening really is. In rehab, you're talking to 30 damaged people. It was really, really important that you did listen, because that was the difference between them going home, or never seeing their four kids again, or killing themselves. It was life or death.'

One of the turning points for Darran was realising that he had got to a stage where not only could he admit that he needed help, he could help others, too. 'The only thing I could do in there was listen. And it was intense. We were talking about serious stuff every day. I remember being in a house meeting once and you would go around and everyone would be asked how they were feeling. There was this one girl, usually quiet as a mouse, but she opened up and shared with the group. I got this strange feeling, like when you're watching a film and you think you're going to start crying. I couldn't figure out why. Then I realised it was because I had been speaking to her about this sort of thing, trying to help her come out of her shell and tell her that it was alright to speak up for herself. And here she was, doing it. She had this big grin on her face; she was made up with herself. I'm there trying not to cry, rubbing my eyes and looking away. The only time I used to cry was when I was really pissed. I realised I wasn't just this empty vessel, and that maybe I had made a difference in some way, just by being there and helping her work through something. To see the change in her was amazing. Even now, when days are pretty bad, I still think back to that time because I don't want to ever lose sight of that. Doing shifts at Samaritans puts me back in that mindset, where it's not all about me. It's about other people who need help.

'Every time I pick up the phone now on a shift at Samaritans, I could be speaking to someone in the same kind of situation that I was in. I never forget who I'm talking to. I never forget what a privilege it is to be let in. Because I know how difficult it is for someone to let it out. It can take someone dozens of attempts to try and say what it is they want to say. I don't mind as long as they're there and they've had the bottle to pick up the phone. I've got to give them my full concentration, because what goes on in that next half an hour, or even just the next 10 minutes, can really change someone's life.'

It's been four-and-a-half years since Darran left rehab and, although he's still on a journey, he feels comfortable with where he's at. 'It took a long, long time to get here. I still do have days that are tough. But I've learned some really important lessons and with my work at Samaritans, I'm still learning. It is a real honour to be part of someone's journey, to sit with them when it's tough.'

Listening has been an invaluable part of Darran's life. When he reflects back on his journey, he realises how it was never the case that someone else could fix him, or tell him what to do. He needed to work it out in his own way – because it was always down to him which path to take. 'No one else could do it for me. And that's how I progressed. I needed to be broken down and then built back up as me.'

How to listen from afar

There is huge value in authentic human connection – however you communicate that. Giving time, undivided attention and empathy meets a fundamental emotional need.

Even if you live far away from the person you're supporting, or you can't see them face to face, it doesn't mean you can't be there for them. Using video chats, phone calls, texts and emails can still help you listen to someone from afar. They can also help if the person you're supporting can't find the right words straight away. Just keeping in regular contact shows you care.

During the 2020 COVID-19 pandemic, I volunteered for Samaritans throughout lockdown. Callers talked about feeling lonely, missing their families, and shared worries about finances and unemployment. There was concern about what life would look like when restrictions were lifted. Over lockdown, people had more time to think. They might have found themselves obsessing about relationships that had gone wrong, or thinking about friends and family they'd lost, and getting very sad. With social interaction limited, people recognised how much they appreciated those close to them and might have phoned or emailed – even if they hadn't been in touch for a while. In some ways, having this time encouraged us to communicate with one another on a deeper level. At the height of lockdown, when we were physically isolated, it seemed to become more important than ever to stay connected. We found all sorts of ways of doing that: a text, a call, a Zoom get-together or a handwritten card meant so much.

What most people missed most was human contact. We are social animals who crave closeness, but we were being robbed of the freedom to interact. It was really hard not being able to visit relatives, hug one another, or celebrate important occasions in a group. Only when they were gone, did we see how much we'd taken these precious things for granted.

As for life going forwards, I think people really intend to hold on to the new sense of balance we've experienced: working a few days from home, for example, and not being tied to a desk, a punishing commute, or a rigid work schedule. We're pledging not to fly quite so much or buy so many unnecessary things. Post-pandemic, we want to retain the qualities of consideration and kindness towards others. In the same way that listening seems a simple concept that can do huge and powerful things; so, too, can showing care, and being kind and honest about how we are feeling.

Talking through issues with friends and family can follow the same conversational arc as a Samaritans phone call. It might begin with raised emotions and possibly even confrontation, but once feelings have been aired and talked through, things begin to calm down. Then you can say, 'You mentioned this, do you want to tell me a bit more about it?' or, 'You seem to have a great deal going on at the moment; what's troubling you most?' That encourages the person to unpick the pile of worries that's going round and round in their head. Once you start to come down the other side of the arc, you might say something like, 'What will you do when this phone call has ended?' or 'What does the rest of the evening look like for you?' It's about encouraging them to see that there's a way forwards, a future.

During lockdown, I spoke to friends who were missing work – the buzz of the office – or their grandchildren. One friend, who is usually the life and soul, fell into such a deep depression he could barely communicate for several days. By using open questions, gently asking him how he was feeling, we found a way through. He was someone who'd led a very successful life, but suddenly the pandemic and its restrictions were beyond his control. It affected him deeply, but simply listening, clarifying and reflecting back what he was saying – along with walks in the fresh air when he felt able – had amazing results.

If a person is feeling lonely, misunderstood or isolated, sensing that someone cares and is prepared to listen can be transformative. For anyone reaching out to someone who is struggling, remember that it doesn't matter what you say; just saying something is so much better than saying nothing. You don't even need to be a deeply empathetic person; anyone can do this. You don't need to get too deep and emotional; just say, 'Hey, are you OK?'

The pandemic has shown us that our mental health is as important as our physical health. Now, it's up to us to shape what comes next.

Sue, Samaritans listening volunteer

Kindness and connection can make all the difference

Jonny Benjamin MBE is a British mental health campaigner and author. He was born in London to a conservative Jewish family. He first visited a psychologist at the age of five. From that young age, Jonny felt as if seeing his psychologist was a secret, remembering: 'Most people didn't have the language or the confidence to talk about it when I was growing up.' As a result, he kept his head down and just tried to get through school, while always feeling conscious that he was ·very different from everyone else. But the feeling of secrecy around expressing his emotions stayed with him and, over time, his secret came to feel like a burden.

At around the age of 10, Jonny was also struggling with his sexuality. Coming from a Jewish background and going to a faith school, neither mental health nor sexuality was ever talked about, let alone taught about. Looking back, Jonny says he hid a lot of himself, particularly when he started to really suffer in his mid-teens.

'I had really low moods and mood swings from the age of 15, and was often very tearful for no reason,' he says. This might seem like normal teenage behaviour, but then Jonny developed psychosis, where he thought he was being told to do or stop doing things by a voice that only he could hear. But because of the sense of secrecy and shame surrounding his feelings and psychological behaviours, he didn't feel like he could tell anyone what was going on. 'I just didn't understand any of it, but I thought I was being told to do things or else I would be punished, or someone I love would be punished.

I put it down to religion, and a close connection to God. But then, when I started really struggling with my mental health and my sexuality, I felt that it was the opposite, that it was the voice of the devil, and because I didn't understand what was happening, I thought it was because I was a bad person. I just kept quiet and covered everything up.'

For years, Jonny coped alone, feeling like he couldn't tell anyone about what was going on. And because he was doing so well academically and appeared to be so high-functioning on the outside, no one knew how much he was struggling on the inside. Using his studies as escapism, he excelled academically, which added an extra burden when maintaining the appearance that everything was fine.

When Jonny was 17, he began to have suicidal feelings, and so, without telling his parents, he went to the doctor and said, 'What is going on? You have to help me.'

'I knew that something was wrong and I didn't want to tell my family because of the weight of expectation that was on me. I'm not criticising my family at all. They didn't have any education around mental health themselves, so how could they help? And so I just tried to push through. I kept telling myself I'd go away to university in Manchester, leave all my issues behind at home in London and there would be a new me. I had this belief that I would be able to run away from everything.

'But actually, going away to university was really hard. I didn't leave anything behind at home. Everything in my head came with me. But there was an added pressure and expectation, not just about academics, but also the idea that I had to have a brilliant time. My mental health really deteriorated. I could hide more easily. I started self-harming and misusing alcohol – things that I might not have been able to hide from my parents if I was at home. I struggled more and more and again, went in secret to my student doctor, who tried me on different antidepressants. But I just gradually became more and more isolated; I internalised everything. I felt as though I had all these secrets, and the longer they stayed with me, the worse I felt, to the point that it became completely unbearable.'

By his third year of university, Jonny's issues had been building up and he was using coping mechanisms like drinking too much to try and push the bad feelings away. 'But one night, I felt like I was being completely taken over; I thought I was possessed. I wasn't talking in my own language, and it escalated and escalated until I found myself on the streets screaming and shouting at people, and then I ended up on the dual carriageway. It was horrible. It was really frightening, but I think I'd just dissociated from what I was doing. It was as if 90 per cent of me was saying these words, but the rest of me recognised that I needed to stop and get out of that situation.'

Jonny was admitted to a psychiatric hospital, where he stayed for six weeks. He was diagnosed with schizoaffective disorder and put on suicide watch. 'The medicalised model is so concerned with looking at behaviour and symptoms, then diagnosis, which leads to medication and therapy, which gets you well enough to be out of the system. There is, of course, room for the correct diagnosis and medication, and that is really important. But my experience was so medical – it felt very medication-obsessed. I wanted to be heard, but my psychiatrist would come and see me every morning for two minutes and talk at me, but in those circumstances he wasn't able to listen.'

Jonny ran away from the hospital and ended up in a situation where he felt like he couldn't go on any longer. 'I just felt like I had nothing left. I'd been given this diagnosis. I felt like I was going to be in the hospital forever. I couldn't come out about my sexuality. It just felt like there was no point.'

While in the process of attempting to take his own life, he was interrupted by a stranger – and the story has since become a book about his journey from despair to hope.

One of the immediate things that struck Jonny when the stranger approached him was that he didn't feel judged. 'This guy came along, and he was just like "OK, this is alright." He didn't try to fix the situation or push it away. It was just OK. He was totally OK with where I was at, and I'd never experienced that before. It was so different to being in the hospital, where people didn't seem to have the time to listen to me. He was so kind. He just said, "I'm not going anywhere; I'm going to stay with you." I'd spent so much time with psychiatrists saying to me and to my parents, "We don't know what's going to happen to Jonny," but this guy just said, "You can get through this." There were lots of gaps and pauses in the conversation where he was just there. I hadn't experienced that, being in a hospital where people didn't have time and you're seen for two minutes. He gave me time and I didn't have to fill the space. He just kind of joined me in it and was there, and he just listened. It felt so different. I don't even remember everything he said. It was just chat about where he grew up, that he was off to work later. Nothing more than that.'

Jonny had an overwhelming feeling that maybe there was a different way to get through what he was experiencing. 'It was such a revelation that someone was OK with me, and he wasn't judging me at all. He just wanted me to talk to him. He wasn't afraid, he wasn't embarrassed. For a complete stranger to give me so much time, it made me feel worthy of being alive. If he had the faith in me to believe I could keep going, then maybe I could have that faith in myself, too. It gave me a new outlook. It gave me a sense of hope.'

Jonny was taken to a local hospital before being sent back to the one he had run away from. Nothing had changed. He looked around and saw the same people from before, that were still so ill, and didn't seem to be getting any better. But something inside him had changed. He had the same treatment, the same care, he was put back on suicide watch – but he describes a new sense of hope that made him see everything differently. 'I knew I didn't want to be there anymore. I thought to myself, I can get through this. That conversation with a total stranger had such a massive impact in terms of changing my perspective. It was like a catalyst.'

When he came out of hospital, Jonny went into his local Samaritans branch to talk to someone there. 'That feeling of being listened to was so amazing. It was so different to having a ten-minute slot with the GP, or hearing a diagnosis from someone. Even with a private therapist, there's a feeling that every second counts. And in day-to-day life, everyone's always so busy, rushing around, but when I'm sitting down with a Samaritan, they have time. To have someone's complete, undivided focus and attention is really powerful. There's no desk, no notebook – no barrier. You're just having a conversation. It's not oppressive. It's a neutral space and it felt like we were just two people on an equal level. Even now, if I need to talk to someone, I go into a branch, as my confidence to talk one-to-one has improved. I feel like I really need that in-person support when I'm in a difficult, dark place: it can really help you develop a stronger connection. Experiencing how kind and warm and non-judgemental someone could be was so reassuring. By removing confrontation and formality, you create a safe space where you're doing nothing more than just having a conversation and answering questions without being disturbed. That, in itself, is really rare and unique.'

Jonny also began to talk to his friends and family more about what he was going through. 'I feel like I came out twice in a way – once to tell my family and friends I'm gay, and once about my mental health. It's been a journey in building up our confidence and understanding how to be able to talk about things and not be scared of these sorts of conversations. Initially, it was really difficult to talk to my dad about it. He just didn't have the language. I didn't have the language either. But when I was discharged from the hospital, I became an outpatient. He would drive me to my hospital appointments and then drive me back afterwards. It was during those car journeys we were able to have really difficult conversations. We probably still have our best talks when we're in the car. There's just that thing of not having to look someone in the eye.'

Jonny has also seen these kinds of conversations evolve with his family and friends over the years. 'I remember one night when I was really struggling a few years ago, and I was out to dinner with a group of good male friends. I wanted them to know I was suffering, so I told them what I was going through. There was a really awkward silence, then someone just said, "Oh, should we get the bill?" But now, when I do the same thing and tell my friends over dinner that I'm having a hard time, they just say, "Oh, OK. I'm sorry to hear it." And that's really validating. Even if they can't relate, or don't quite know what to say, it makes me feel like I'm not abnormal, and just having a friend or family member say "It's alright" takes away the shame and the guilt. It just goes to show how people can evolve and change.'

Jonny's advice on making authentic connections

- We all have it within ourselves to reach out to another person, human to human and ask if they're OK. There's no special formula. It's just about being human. You can do it.

- It's not about having the right words, it's about just being there during that painful or difficult time, in solidarity, in the same way you would stay with someone if they'd had a physical accident or injury.

- Being side by side can be great for opening up. Go for a walk or a drive.

- Keep trying. For the first, second or third time, it might not work, but regular contact can chip away and let you know someone is there for you and that they care.

- There might be a gap or a silence that feels uncomfortable, but it's amazing how well just letting people have the time and space to say what they need to works – and that can be really liberating.

- You don't need to have an agenda. You don't need to worry about how you respond. You don't need to fix anything. People can be their own guides. They just need to realise they can. Give people credit for their own ability to heal.

Supporting someone you don't know

While this book is designed with friends, family, loved ones and colleagues in mind, it might also be helpful to understand what to do if you see someone you don't know who seems to be in danger of harming themselves. Suicide is preventable and thoughts of taking your own life are often temporary, and can be interrupted. A simple question or observation can be all it takes to interrupt a negative thought cycle and start someone on the journey to recovery.

There's no right or wrong way to approach someone. Trust your instincts. If you think somebody looks withdrawn, distant or upset and as if they might need help, strike up a conversation; remember that you chat with people every day. You can't make things worse simply by asking if someone is OK. If you don't feel it's safe to make an approach, or you don't feel comfortable doing so you can always alert a passer-by, or there might be a professional such as a member of staff nearby. If not, you can call 999.

What to say or do if you approach someone:

- 'It's a warm evening, isn't it?'
- 'What's your name?'
- 'Do you need any help?'
- 'Are you OK?'
- Introduce yourself – tell the person where you're going and what you're doing.
- Ask the person if there's someone you can call for them.
- Ask them if they want to sit down somewhere and get a hot drink.
- You could mention sources of help, including Samaritans and their GP, as well as friends and family.

Just letting them know someone is there can help.

'Remember to look up
at the stars and not down
at your feet. Try to make sense
of what you see and wonder about
what makes the universe exist.
Be curious. And however difficult
life may seem, there is always
something you can do and
succeed at. It matters that
you don't just give up.'

Stephen Hawking

Chapter 11:
Self-care when supporting others

You can't pour from an empty jug

Being there for other people isn't always easy. Listening to someone you know and care about who is struggling can be challenging and overwhelming, particularly if they are talking about sensitive or difficult topics. Remember that you can't pour from an empty jug. Continually giving care to others but forgetting to treat yourself with kindness and compassion will leave you feeling drained, which can lead to tiredness and irritability.

If you're under a lot of stress, it can affect your judgement and that can mean you're not able to have the conversation that you need to in a meaningful way. It's important to have a safety network. At Samaritans, before you go on a shift you check in with your shift leader, and afterwards, you have a short debrief, to process your experience and talk about your feelings.

Kindness to the self is just as important as kindness to others. So take time for yourself, to recharge and refill. Remember the in-flight safety instructions? You must put your own oxygen mask on first before helping anyone else fit theirs – because how can you look after someone else if you don't look after yourself?

Managing your emotions and reactions

It's not always easy to put your own feelings aside and listen to someone you care about without overreacting or feeling like you need to take on the weight of their issues. If you feel you aren't able to react sensitively to a situation, it might be helpful to take a few moments to think about things more generally, such as your relationship with the person, the difficulties they are facing, and what's worrying you. This can help you get some perspective and help you to feel more in control of the situation.

As well as being aware of how you react, be aware of pushing aside your own emotions so that you can focus your energy on the person you're talking to. Although part of active listening is focusing on the other person and not making it all about you or bringing up your own experiences or opinions, suppressing your own feelings could have consequences later on, especially if you're trying to quash feelings of grief, stress or anger. So try and take note of how you are feeling and find ways of dealing with your emotions in your own time, rather than ignoring or suppressing them. You might do this by talking to another person who you trust, or giving yourself time to do something you enjoy. If you are supporting someone and finding it difficult, it may be helpful to find someone who can be there for you, too.

Try to build up a support network

No one can give another person everything they need, especially through difficult times. It's important to manage your own expectations, as well as theirs, about what is a practical amount of support for you to give. Otherwise you may start feeling you are letting them down or failing.

Try and get other friends or family members involved to share the responsibility if it feels like too much for you to do alone. This will take the pressure off you and help the person you're supporting get more of the help they need to feel better.

Talk to someone, too

Hearing about how difficult things are for people that you know and love can be a big shock, especially if they've been keeping it to themselves for a long time. It's OK to be honest about being surprised or not knowing what to say. Remember that if someone wants to talk to you, you do not need to take their burden on to your shoulders. This doesn't mean you can't share a person's worries. It's understandable for you to be upset if someone you care about has told you something very sad or upsetting. In this situation, it's important to find someone you can trust to talk things through with afterwards. Don't carry difficult feelings around with you – it's important that you offload, too.

You do not need to fix their issue. Just being there and listening can be more helpful than anything. But it's OK to recognise when you don't have the capacity to deal with anything beyond your own daily life and it's important not to feel bad about that. Taking time out or helping someone seek alternative care can be really helpful. See page 179 for more about deciding whether you are the right person to listen.

Make sure you look after yourself, too

My experience at Samaritans was very different to that of being a psychotherapist. The call to Samaritans was usually when someone was at crisis point. That doesn't always mean that they were suicidal, but it does mean they were at a tipping point in loneliness or depression and had taken the brave step of contacting Samaritans to show their interest in changing their situation. As a psychotherapist, you work with someone over a longer period of time, so you develop a therapeutic relationship – you get underneath the crisis and start to find a longer-term, sustainable solution. Often the call to Samaritans is the first critical step in the road to recovery.

Being a good listener begins with self-love. It begins at home – with a comfort in yourself. You can feel that you are technically 'listening', i.e. not talking over the person, not planning your reply while they're still speaking, and all of those practical tips, but for me, to really be a good listener we need to sort out our own 'stuff'. In this way, we avoid projecting our stories on to the other person. Too often, rather than looking after our own issues we take on someone else as a project and want to fix them, trying to tell them what they should do. Learning to listen to ourselves is the first step in becoming a better listener: listening to our bodies and knowing and doing what we need to when exhausted or stressed to ensure we give ourselves the time out to reflect.

By attending to our own fears, anxieties and struggles, we can be in a better place to support others. For example, if you are unhappy in your relationship and a friend comes to you wanting to talk about a relationship issue, it can be easy to project your own relationship problems on to your friend. These are feelings and actions that perhaps you need to take account of in your own self; your own life. If we are really listening, we avoid our own dilemmas from spilling over.

The important thing to bear in mind when listening to a friend or family member's deep concerns is that you need to surround yourself with a team. Helping by listening can't just be one person's responsibility. Help the person who is revealing their feelings explore who else they can talk to, either together with you or independently. Explore, with them, who else you can make aware, who else can be part of your support team, and build this team with the person's knowledge and permission.

Listening and hearing distressing revelations can be scary (and even triggering for issues in your past – see page 179). It's even harder when you are the parent, partner, friend or work colleague. The fact that this person is sharing with you is a really positive thing – they are taking a really brave step. Sharing this with you takes real courage, which you should acknowledge. There is real hope in a cry for help, as it shows there is trust and a desire to get out of situation.

UKCP psychotherapist Hilda Burke volunteered for Samaritans for over a decade before retraining as a psychotherapist.

Self-care action plan

Who can you talk to?
Note down the details of people who can help you if you find yourself needing to talk to someone.

Their name: ....

Phone number: ....

Notes: ....
(e.g. when can ....
you call them?
How good are ....
they at listening/ ....
supporting?) ....

Things that help you relax
Collect and list the things that help you relax, or that inspire you and give you hope. This could be things you love, things you're looking forward to, or anything else that you find uplifting.

What are the things that help you relax?
....
....

What inspires you?
....
....

Add something that gives you hope in a sentence:
....
....

Self check-in

Use this space to write down any signs you can recognise that might mean you want to talk to someone. This can include:

• thoughts and images
• thinking styles (e.g. rumination/repetitive thoughts, thinking biases such as catastrophising, 'all or nothing' thinking)
• changes in your mood
• feelings of shame or guilt
• changes in habits or behaviours (e.g. sleeping poorly, feeling exhausted, being tearful or arguing more with family)

....
....
....
....
....
....
....
....
....
....
....
....
....
....
....
....

Practice wellbeing

Here are some tips and suggestions about how to practise self-care and take some time out to look after yourself. You can also suggest them as ideas for the person you are supporting.

How to look after yourself

• Keep to a regular routine.
• Sleep well.
• Eat healthily.
• Exercise.
• Reward yourself for any achievements.
• Find something that helps you relax.
• Avoid indulgence in stimulants, such as caffeine and alcohol.

Be active

Exercise is essential for wellbeing, but it doesn't need to be particularly intense for you to feel good – slower-paced activities, such as walking, can have the benefit of encouraging social interactions as well as providing some level of exercise. Here are a few ideas for getting physical.

• Take the stairs, not the lift.
• Go for a walk at lunchtime, or get off the bus one stop earlier than usual and walk the final part of your journey.
• Do some gardening.
• Join a local gym or swimming pool.
• Organise a sporting activity in your local community, or at work or with your friends.
• Have a kick-about in a local park.
• Put on some music and have a kitchen disco.
• Go for a bike ride.
• Choose a regular fitness activity that suits your level of fitness, from a cycle or run to yoga or a gentle stretch.

Take some time to enjoy the moment and the environment around you

Being aware of what is taking place in the present directly enhances your wellbeing, and savouring the moment can help to reaffirm your life priorities. Heightened awareness also enhances your self-understanding and allows you to make positive choices based on your own values and motivations. Here are a few ideas.

• Take a moment to be aware of your surroundings.
• Get a plant for your workspace.
• Have a 'clear the clutter' day.
• Visit a new café for lunch.
• Take notice of how your friends, family, loved ones and colleagues are feeling or acting.
• Practise mindfulness.

Learn

Continued learning throughout life enhances self-esteem and encourages social interaction and a more active lifestyle. The practice of setting goals is strongly associated with higher levels of wellbeing. Why not learn something new today?

• Try out a new recipe.
• Sign up for a class.
• Read the news or a book – or even set up a book club.
• Do a crossword or Sudoku.
• Learn to play an instrument.
• Research something you've always wondered about.
• Learn a new word.

Give

Participation in social and community life can be great for wellbeing. Giving back and performing an act of kindness can really improve someone's mood.

- Smile at a stranger.
- Become a volunteer.
- Cook a meal and take it to a friend.
- Donate to a charity shop.
- Make a gift for someone.

Relax

- Listen to music.
- Do some journalling.
- Have a bath.
- Do some mindful colouring.
- Light a scented candle.
- Read a good book
- Practise meditation.

Connect with others

Feeling close to – and valued by – other people is a fundamental human need and one that contributes to emotional wellbeing. Social relationships are critical for acting as a buffer against mental ill health for people of all ages. So take time to connect with friends, loved ones, family members, colleagues and neighbours. You can do this at work, at home, in school or as part of your local community.

- Talk to someone instead of sending an email.
- Speak to someone new.
- Ask how someone's weekend or evening was and really listen when they tell you.
- Join a community group.
- Give a colleague a lift to work or share the journey home with them.

It's OK to ask for help

We all went through a very strange time during the COVID-19 pandemic. I unfortunately lost my father, who passed away suddenly in Spain. Thankfully, I made it over there to bring him home before lockdown. Every single one of us had our own issues during those incredibly difficult times, from those who live alone to those with existing mental health conditions. Now, more than ever, we need to remain connected to one another.

I've been very vocal about my mental health problems. I can remember calling the Samaritans number time after time, trying to get the confidence to speak, but I would hang up, as I was ashamed of how I felt. The time I did stay on the phone was one of the best days of my life. Someone listened. They asked no questions, they didn't need my name. I cried, I talked, and when I put down the phone, many hours later, I knew I was not alone. The person on the other end of the line helped me more than I can ever explain.

We all have problems, small issues, things you worry about that you don't want to concern others with. But we need to voice our feelings and share what's going on with friends and family. We need to say it out loud. You would be surprised how many people are going through what you are going through. Talk. Know that there is always someone there. Be kind to yourself. One little phone call can help so much.

Now, with my ongoing anxiety, I am reassured that someone is always there if I need them. Not only Samaritans volunteers, but the friends I used to be afraid to tell how I was feeling on the inside. There is always someone there. Never ever forget that, no matter how different, lonely, sad or lost you feel. You are never alone.

We can get through anything. Believe me.

Gail Porter, Samaritans Ambassador

Chapter 12:
Next steps

Consider whether you are the right person to listen

They might need to talk to someone else

Sometimes, it is best for an individual to talk to someone outside of their immediate relationship or family, and it's essential to not be offended by that. Their decision to seek support elsewhere isn't a negative comment about your relationship. People instinctively want to protect their loved ones, and it can be that love and desire to protect that makes them more comfortable talking to someone outside of their immediate circle.

The important thing is being open and honest enough with friends, family members, loved ones and colleagues, to be able to begin a conversation about seeking further help should they need to take that approach. Having good conversations with one another and listening to each other is vital, but it's also good to recognise that you might not always be the right person to listen – and that's OK.

You might not be in a position to listen

If you are going through a difficult time, or you have things that are overwhelming in your own life, think about whether you are the right person to offer support. There may be a risk that you start feeling the pressure of someone else's problems on top of your own, or it could make it harder for you to think clearly about how to respond and react to what someone is telling you. If this is the case, it's OK for you to take a step back and perhaps help them find support elsewhere.

It's also possible that you may not be able to support someone if whatever they need to talk about relates to something that could be triggering for you, perhaps due to a past trauma. If this happens, it's important that you prioritise your wellbeing and gently explain to the person that you may not be able to listen. You can try and say something like: 'I'm so sorry you're going through this, and I want to be there for you. I don't want to make this about me, but I have to tell you that I've been through something similar myself and I'm concerned that it means I'm not the right person to talk to you as it could be distressing for both of us. Instead, can I help you find someone who would be able to listen to you in a way that's going to really focus on you and help you feel properly heard?'

When someone needs specialist help

UKCP Psychotherapist Andy Ryan specialises in drug and alcohol treatment services in Yorkshire and the North East

There are certain situations where more specialist help will be needed, for example, for diagnosable mental illnesses, disorders or addictions, such as alcoholism, anorexia, bipolar, PTSD or grief, to name but a few.

Addiction

Addiction is often a dissociation and displacement reaction to trauma or grief in someone's life. When listening to someone who is sharing a problem with addiction, it is most important to keep the conversation open and to be there for them, but also to ensure that the focus is not just on the substances. We need to be able to talk about addiction differently and not so much ask about what substances they are using, but why they are using them. This can be difficult to do within family dynamics, so it is important to be able to pick up the phone and speak to someone in your local community, for example the drug and alcohol treatment services (see page 187).

It might be challenging to hear a loved one talk about their problems with addiction, so ask yourself whether you feel comfortable enough to have the conversation. Know this is a long-term process and you are or should be just one part of this person's support team. Make sure not everything is centred around the issue; ensure you are having human conversations, too. Recognise that when a person changes the subject, it doesn't mean they don't want to talk; it may just mean they have processed enough for now. A lot of people will use shadow humour to cope and as a way of slowly opening up about their pain. In some cases, when people begin to realise the impact of their addictive behaviour on themselves and others, a process of blame can emerge to displace responsibility for difficult realisations.

For sustainable change, we need to create safe spaces for people to recover. At alcohol treatment centres, we don't focus on just the symptoms (rough sleeping, substance use and criminal convictions, for example). We see many of these issues as adaptations and consequences of some difficulties experienced in life. It is important to focus on the whole person, their journey and their trauma to help build a therapeutic alliance and create a safe space for people to share their authentic selves, which can allow them to make meaningful and long-lasting changes if they wish to.

Many people don't know help exists, from addiction support to specific mental health services. As a listener, you can help the other person find access to this support. Encourage them to reach out to their GP. Reaching out for help can be extremely hard due to a fear of being judged, as the addiction process is very hidden and can be layered with shame, guilt and remorse. Most local authority health commissioners have wonderful mental health and addiction resources and a graded system to help you access the right support at the right time. If you are helping someone, there can be many mutual aid groups in your local areas supporting people around differing addictions, but it's also a good idea to look up what your local authority has to offer on their website. This is where you'll find information on local talking therapies, resources, volunteer groups, support groups for drug and alcohol rehabilitation, crisis teams and a whole process to raise concerns if the person you care about isn't getting the support they need.

When just listening might not be enough

Hilda Burke, UKCP psychotherapist and former Samaritans listening volunteer

If you've listened to someone you care about express thoughts and feelings that relate to specific issues or diagnosable mental health issues, there are organisations and resources that can offer specialised support (see pages 187–92 for a detailed list). It's not your job to diagnose, or be an expert, but you can try and help someone understand that there is support available to them and that they might need care.

Trauma

In some cases, for example if someone is dealing with trauma, it can be really challenging to listen to what they have been through. Importantly, it might not actually be helpful for the person you're listening to to repeat the trauma by describing it to you. Traditional listening, which allows a person to relive an experience, can be too hard in this situation – both on you and the person you're supporting. If someone starts to share about trauma, try not to probe for detail as you would when they're talking about other things, like depression. Instead, offer positive ideas, framed as a choice for them to consider, such as 'Have you considered a support group or therapy or speaking to your GP?' This may help them to find a space where they can explore their trauma safely and with specialist support.

Helping them seek further support

Pay attention to the person's tone. If they seem to be speaking from a place of desperation or helplessness, or there's bleakness in their words and the way they are sharing their feelings, it is important to both listen and gently encourage them to seek support. One way to do this is to ask them how they feel about the idea of support, e.g.: 'Do you feel it might be worth a call to your GP? How do you feel about getting support? Do you think speaking to a therapist might help?' Notice that instead of saying 'Will you speak to your GP?' a softer question is more effective – 'Do you feel it might be worth a call to your GP?' In this way, you identify with their feelings, not just the action of asking for help, and place them in a position of control.

What if they refuse support?

Think about what other gently open questions you can ask, for example: 'What is the alternative?' and 'Do you want this situation to change?' By asking the question kindly, you let the person you are listening to have the power. Remember, some people would rather stay feeling miserable than face difficult questions or challenges. While this is hard to hear, when we are talking about adults, we have to respect their own choices and free will. Ultimately, they do have the right to decide if they want to access help or not.

What kind of help is available?

When you hear real desperation in someone's voice, there could be need for immediate support. Samaritans, NHS 111, and your local hospital A&E are 24/7 services that may be able to help – and, if it's an emergency or you think the situation is unsafe, you can call 999.

Calling Samaritans can be a way of getting urgent, essential and immediate emotional support, but it's not continuous, ongoing care. The majority of people will need more healing to address the root cause, and this is where therapists and GPs come in, to provide support in the longer term.

If the way the person is feeling is part of a long-term recurring pattern, and there is no immediate danger to life, then it is generally more appropriate for them to reach out to their GP or to a psychotherapist. Their GP can get them on to an NHS referral list for therapy and low-cost/free counselling. Like most things in life, if they can afford it, they will have greater choice if they can seek psychotherapy privately. It's now possible to choose how we access therapy, our preferred modality (type of therapy) and even which therapist we wish to work with.

Sometimes it isn't a choice of one or the other – different kinds of care can be complementary. All can be lifesaving – and life-changing – in different situations. It's about building a team, which can start with a friend or loved one, a colleague or a Samaritan, and then might grow to involve a GP and a psychotherapist. Part of the journey is listening to what someone needs in order to recover and supporting them on their path.

Conclusion: Over to you

Opening up and being there for someone not only allows us to support each other when they're going through a difficult time; it also helps us challenge the stigma around mental health. We've come a long way from where we were even five to ten years ago, but there's still quite a hill to climb. The more we can demonstrate that it's OK to speak out about how we're feeling, the better.

Day to day, it's about keeping a close connection with the people who are important to you and showing them that you care, then being sensitive enough to recognise when people do need to talk or want to open up and share how they are feeling. What this means is that, in their more difficult moments, that person will trust that they can come to you and tell you what's going on with them. Your job then is to just keep them talking while you listen, in confidence and without judgement. Remember: don't be afraid of silence, and keep your opinions under wraps, unless they are asked for. And don't be afraid of getting it wrong. You have the ability to make a change that could really help someone.

Often, the simplest acts are the most meaningful. In all those months of psychiatric care, the turning point for Steven was the auxiliary nurse who gave him a cheerful hello every day. For Jonny, it was a moment of connection with a passer-by he'd never met before. For Darran, it was the new alcohol support worker who directed the question back to him. For a lot of people, it's been an anonymous call with a Samaritans volunteer. These moments are what gave them hope to begin their journey of recovery: not the clinical fix, the diagnosis, the medication, but the moment of feeling validated and heard.

The challenge now is to look to the future. As the way people choose to communicate changes over time, Samaritans – and society – will continue to evolve, combining technology with compassion, to reach out and be there for one another in new and different ways. As the world changes, we too must invest in new ways of making sure we can reach out to those around us. Our aim at Samaritans is to make sure there's someone there for anyone who needs them. Your role is to extend that arm of support to those around you. You don't need to save anyone. Just be there to stand alongside them until they are ready to save themselves.

The Samaritans listening model

• Use open questions: How? What? Where? Who?

• Summarise: A summary helps to show the individual that you have listened to and understood their circumstances and their feelings.

• Reflect: Repeating back a word or phrase encourages the individual to carry on and expand.

• Clarify: Sometimes an individual may gloss over an important point. By exploring these areas further, you can help them clarify these points for themselves.

• Use short words of encouragement: The person may need help to go on with their story – use words or phrases like 'yes' or 'go on'.

• React: We need to show that we have understood the situation by reacting to it with validating phrases like 'That sounds very difficult'.

'[Hope is] not just optimism – hope is something that is there to be worked for, is worth working for, and can work.'

Seamus Heaney

Where to seek further support

Samaritans

You can get in touch with Samaritans to talk about anything that's troubling you, no matter how large or small the issue feels. You can get free, confidential emotional support at any time by calling our 24-hour listening service on 116 123, or emailing us at jo@samaritans.org. The number won't show up on your bill. Please also visit www.samaritans.org for online chat and our self-help guidance.

If you're looking for advice or specialist support for a particular issue, these organisations may be able to help.

ADDICTION

Alcoholics Anonymous
For anyone with a desire to tackle their own drink problem.
alcoholics-anonymous.org.uk

Al-Anon
Offers understanding and support for families and friends of problem drinkers in an anonymous environment, whether the alcoholic is still drinking or not.
Tel: 0800 0086 811
www.al-anonuk.org.uk
Tel: 01 873 2699 – Republic of Ireland
al-anon-ireland.org – Republic of Ireland

Dan 24/7 (Wales)
Support with drug and alcohol problems.
Tel: 0808 808 2234
Text: 81066
dan247.org.uk

Drinkline
UK-wide helpline for anyone concerned about their alcohol use or someone else's.
Tel: 0300 123 1110
drinkaware.co.uk/alcohol-support-services

Drugs.ie (Republic of Ireland)
Provides support, information, guidance and referral to anyone with a question or concern related to drug and alcohol use and/or HIV and sexual health.
Tel: 1800 459 459 (Freephone)
drugs.ie

Dunlewey Addiction Services (N. Ireland)
Confidential counselling and mentoring programme for those experiencing difficulties with their own, or other people's substance misuse or gambling issues.
Tel: 028 9039 2547
Tel: 0800 886 725
dunlewey.net

Frank
Friendly, confidential drugs advice.
Tel: 0300 123 6600
Text: 82111
talktofrank.com

Gamblers Anonymous
Group meeting support at locations around the country for those who wish to recover from gambling addiction.
Tel: 0330 094 0322
gamblersanonymous.org.uk
Tel: 01 872 1133 – Republic of Ireland
gamblersanonymous.ie – Republic of Ireland

GamCare
*Information, advice, support and free
counselling for the prevention and treatment
of problem gambling.*
Tel: 0808 802 0133
gamcare.org.uk

Know the Score (Scotland)
Free, confidential information about drugs.
Tel: 0333 230 9468
gamcare.org.uk

BENEFITS AND RIGHTS

Citizens Advice
*Impartial advice on rights and responsibilities
across the UK.*
Tel: 0344 411 1444 (England and Wales)
Tel: 0808 800 9060 (Scotland)
Tel: 0344 477 2020 (Welsh Speaker)
Tel: 0800 028 1881 (N. Ireland)
citizensadvice.org.uk

Farming Community Network
*Confidential help and advice to those within
the farming community.*
Tel: 0300 011 1999
Email: help@fcn.org.uk
fcn.org.uk

BEREAVEMENT

Child Bereavement UK
*Support for families when a baby or child of
any age dies or is dying, or when a child is
facing bereavement.*
Tel: 0800 028 8840
Email: support@childbereavementuk.org
childbereavementuk.org

Cruse (England/Scotland)
*Offers support for bereaved people. Also
supports those coping with the death of pets.*
Tel: 0808 808 1677
Tel: 0845 600 2227 - Cruse Scotland
Email: helpline@cruse.org.uk
cruse.org.uk
crusescotland.org.uk - Cruse Scotland

The Irish Hospice Foundation (Rep. of Ireland)
*Offers information and resources to support
bereaved persons. Website provides info re:
Covid-19 including funeral information.*
Tel: 01 679 3188
hospicefoundation.ie/bereavement

CARERS

Carers UK
Support for unpaid carers for family or friends.
Tel: 0808 808 7777 (England, Scotland, Wales)
Tel: 028 9043 9843 (NI)
Email: advice@carersuk.org
carersuk.org

Family Action (England & Wales)
*Provides emotional and practical support
around family pressures.*
Tel: 0808 802 6666
Text: 07537 404 282
Email: familyline@family-action.org.uk
family-action.org.uk

Family Carers Ireland (Republic of Ireland)
*The Carers Association provides a number of
services nationwide, to family carers, which
are aimed at helping to increase the quality of
life for the carer and the person receiving care
at home.*
Tel: 1800 240 724
familycarers.ie

CHILDREN AND YOUNG PEOPLE

ChildLine (18 years and younger)
*Free help and support for children and young
people in the UK.*
Tel: 0800 11 11
childline.org.uk

ChildLine (Republic of Ireland)
*Part of the ISPCC (The Irish Society for the
Prevention of Cruelty to Children)*
Tel: 1800 666 666 (under-18s only; freephone)
Tel: 01 676 7960 (Parents can ring)
Text: 50101 (free text)
childline.ie

Jigsaw (Republic of Ireland)

Jigsaw strives to ensure that no young person feels alone, isolated and disconnected from others around them by providing vital support to young people with their mental health and working closely with communities across Ireland.
Tel: 01 4727 010
jigsaw.ie

The Mix

Free help and support for children and young people aged 25 years and younger in the UK.
Tel: 0808 808 4994
themix.org.uk

CRISIS PREGNANCY

Positive Options (Republic of Ireland)

State-funded organisation that offers a range of crisis pregnancy counselling services to women with a crisis pregnancy and their partners.
Tel: 1800 828 010
Text: 50444 (free text list)
positiveoptions.ie

Pregnancy Crisis Helpline

The Pregnancy Crisis Helpline offers you a safe, confidential place for you to talk about your unplanned pregnancy or previous abortion.
Tel: 0800 368 9296
pregnancycrisishelpline.org.uk

DEBT, POVERTY AND SOCIAL INCLUSION

Citizens Information Board (Rep. of Ireland)

Statutory body which supports the provision of information, advice and advocacy on a broad range of public and social services.
Tel: 0761 07 4000
citizensinformation.ie

MABS (Republic of Ireland)

A national, free, confidential and independent service for people in debt or in danger of getting into debt.
Tel: 0761 07 2000
mabs.ie

Society of St Vincent de Paul

Exists to fight poverty and their network gives practical support to those experiencing poverty and social exclusion by providing a wide range of services to those in need.
Tel: 07587 035 121
svp.org.uk
Tel: 01 884 8200 – Republic of Ireland
svp.ie – Republic of Ireland

StepChange Debt Charity

Comprehensive debt advice for people in the UK.
Tel: 0800 138 1111
stepchange.org

EATING DISORDERS

Anorexia Bulimia Care

Personal care and support for anyone affected by anorexia, bulimia, binge eating and all types of eating distress.
Tel: 0300 011 1213
anorexiabulimiacare.org.uk

B-EAT

Support and information relating to eating disorders.
Tel: 0808 801 0677 (adults over 18)
Email: help@beateatingdisorders.org.uk (adults over 18)
Tel: 0808 801 0711 (youth line under 18)
Email: fyp@beateatingdisorders.org.uk (youth line under 18)
beateatingdisorders.org.uk

Bodywhys (Republic of Ireland)

Provides a range of support services for people affected by eating disorders, including specific services for families and friends.
Tel: 01 210 7906 (Lo-call number)
Email: alex@bodywhys.ie
bodywhys.ie

HEALTH

NHS 111 (England, N. Ireland, Wales & Scotland)
Health advice and reassurance.
Tel: 111
111.nhs.ukhse.ie – Republic of Ireland

HOUSING AND HOMELESSNESS

Shelter (England, Scotland & Wales)/ Housing Rights (NI)
Housing and homelessness charity offering advice and information.
Tel: 0808 800 4444 (England, Scotland)
Tel: 08000 495 495 (Wales)
Tel: 028 9024 5640 (Northern Ireland)
shelter.org.uk

Threshold (Republic of Ireland)
National charity providing independent advisory and advocacy services, working in collaboration with others for those disadvantaged by the housing system. Their aim is to provide long-term solutions for people who are homeless.
Tel: 1800 454 454
threshold.ie

LONELINESS AND ISOLATION

Alone (Republic of Ireland)
Supporting older people who are socially isolated, homeless or living in poverty or crisis. They offer befriending, housing support, support coordination and assistance with technology.
Tel: 081 822 224
Email: hello@alone.ie
alone.ie

Befrienders Worldwide
International charity providing confidential support to people in emotional crisis or distress, or those close to them. It includes a directory of emotional support helplines around the world.
befrienders.org

MENTAL HEALTH

Aware (Northern Ireland)
Confidential helpline and email service for people who are experiencing depression.
Tel: 028 9035 7820 (free in Northern Ireland)
Email: help@aware-ni.org
aware-ni.org

Aware (Republic of Ireland)
The organisation undertakes to create a society where people with depression are understood and supported, are free from stigma, and have access to a broad range of appropriate therapies to enable them to reach their full potential.
aware.ie
Tel: 1800 804 848 (Freephone)

SAMH (Scotland)
Mental health information and signposting to local services. (Not a listening service or suitable for people in crisis.)
Tel: 0141 530 1000
Email: enquire@samh.org.uk
samh.org.uk

TALKING THERAPIES

BACP (British Association for Counselling and Psychotherapy)
BACP is a membership organisation that sets standards for therapeutic practice. Their online directory can be used to locate a professional counsellor, who will usually charge for their services.
Tel: 01455 883300
Email: bacp@bacp.co.uk
bacp.co.uk

Connect Counselling (Republic of Ireland)
Counselling service for any adult who has experienced abuse, trauma or neglect in childhood. The service is also available to partners or relatives of people with these experiences.
Tel: 1800 477 477
connectcounselling.ie

GROW (Republic of Ireland)
A mental health organisation which helps people who have suffered, or are suffering, from mental health problems.
Tel: 1890 474 474
grow.ie

Mind (England and Wales)
Advice, support and information around mental health issues. Mind has a legal advice line in England and Wales.
Tel: 0300 123 3393
Text: 86463
Email: info@mind.org.uk
mind.org.uk

Pieta House (Republic of Ireland)
Provides a specialised treatment programme for people who have suicidal ideation or who engage in self-harming behaviours. They also provide support and help to people bereaved by suicide.
Tel: 1800 247 247
pieta.ie

Shine (Republic of Ireland)
National organisation dedicated to upholding the rights and addressing the needs of all those affected by enduring mental illness including, but not exclusively, schizophrenia, schizo-affective disorder and bipolar disorder, through the promotion and provision of high-quality services.
shine.ie

Shout
Free 24/7 text service support for anyone in crisis and struggling to cope.
Text: 85258
giveusashout.org

UKCP (UK Council for Psychotherapy)
UKCP is the leading body for the training and accreditation of psychotherapists and psychotherapeutic counsellors in the UK. UKCP has over 10,000 members helping to improve lives through support to mental health and emotional wellbeing, both privately and through the NHS and charitable partnerships.
psychotherapy.co.uk

MILITARY

Veterans' Gateway
Veterans' Gateway is the first point of contact for veterans/military personnel and families seeking support.
Tel: 0808 802 1212
Text: 81212
veteransgateway.org.uk

OLDER PEOPLE

Age UK
Support for older people.
Tel: 0800 679 1602 (England)
Tel: 0800 022 3444 (Wales)
Tel: 0800 124 4222* (Scotland)
Tel: 0808 808 7575 (Northern Ireland)
* Age Scotland operates its helpline in partnership with The Silver Line.
ageuk.org.uk

The Silver Line
Information, friendship and advice for older people.
Tel: 0800 470 80 90
thesilverline.org.uk

RELATIONSHIPS

Relate
Counselling and workshops on relationships and family issues.
Tel: 0300 100 1234 (Relate)
Tel: 028 9032 3454 (Relate NI)
Webchat available (check website)
relate.org.uk

Relationships Scotland
Counselling, family mediation and child contact centres.
Tel: 0345 119 2020
relationships-scotland.org.uk

SEXUALITY

Switchboard, the LGBT+ helpline
A safe space for anyone to discuss sexuality, gender identity, sexual health and emotional wellbeing.
Tel: 0300 330 0630
Email: chris@switchboard.lgbt
switchboard.lgbt

LGBT (Republic of Ireland)
Supporting lesbian, gay, bisexual and transgender people and their families.
Tel: 1890 929 539
lgbt.ie

SEXUAL/DOMESTIC ABUSE

Men's Aid (Republic of Ireland) – men only
National service for men experiencing domestic violence in Ireland, supplying support and information.
Tel: 01 554 3811
Email: hello@mensaid.ie
mensaid.ie

Men's Advice Line – men only
Confidential helpline for men experiencing domestic violence in any relationship.
Tel: 0808 801 0327
Email: info@mensadviceline.org.uk
mensadviceline.org.uk

NAPAC (National Association for People Abused in Childhood)
Offers support to adult (18+) survivors of all types of childhood abuse.
Tel: 0800 801 0331
napac.org.uk

Rape Crisis – women only
Tel: 0808 802 9999 (England & Wales)
(12pm–2.30pm and 7–9.30pm every day, and 3–5.30pm weekdays)
Tel: 0808 801 0302 (Scotland) (6pm–12am daily)
Tel: 1800 778 888 (N. Ireland) (24-hour helpline)
rapecrisis.org.uk

Rape Crisis Centre (Republic of Ireland)
Takes calls from women and men of all ages who have experienced or want to talk about the effects of any kind of sexual violence.
Tel: 1800 778 888
drcc.ie

Refuge National Domestic Violence Helpline – (women only)
Support for women experiencing domestic violence (including forced marriages, tech abuse and modern slavery).
Tel: 0808 200 0247
www.nationaldomesticviolencehelpline.org.uk

Women's Aid (Republic of Ireland)
Committed to the elimination of violence and abuse of women through effecting political, cultural and social change. Women's Aid provides direct support services to women experiencing male violence and abuse.
Tel: 1800 341 900
www.womensaid.ie

VICTIMS OF CRIME

Crime Victims Helpline (Republic of Ireland)
Confidential support to victims of crime in Ireland.
Tel: 116006
crimevictimshelpline.ie

Victim Support
Help for victims of crime, witnesses and their families and friends.
Tel: 0808 168 9111 (England, Wales)
Tel: 0800 160 1985 (Scotland)
Tel: 028 9024 3133 (Northern Ireland)
victimsupport.org.uk

AT WORK

Mental Health First Aid England (MHFA)
A social enterprise offering expert guidance and training to support mental health in the workplace and beyond.
mhfaengland.org
mhfaireland.ie